Tina Hartshorne

The Amazing

Life of a Fat

Bird

A Slice Of Turkey

First published in 2020 in paperback form by:

The New Science of Fixing Things Ltd, United Kingdom.

ISBN 979 8 64066 225 2

The Stories

Mutha Fucca Yucca

The Best Rep?

The Holidays

Fakes Anyone?

Just Nipping Down The Road!

Sunflower Tours

Earrings Next Time?

The 'Man'. The Mafia?

Indiana Jones Beat Me To This Place!

A Fishy Tale

Lunch With The Mafia

The Billionaire In A Baseball Cap

A Man's World

Are You In A Safe Place?

Ding Ding!

Dedication

"In everyone's life, at some time, our inner fire goes out. It is then burst into flame by an encounter with another human being. We should all be thankful for those people who rekindle the inner spirit."
— **Albert Schweitzer**

For my best friend, David

I love you to the edge of the observable universe and back

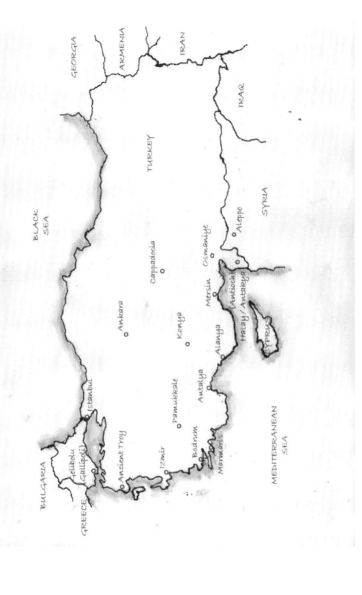

Foreword

Thank you for opening my book. It was written, after years of me saying that there was a book inside me! I have been told, lots of times, that I can tell a good story. The time came when we were all put into lockdown due to Covid 19. I had no more excuses to hide behind, plus my wonderful husband turned into an editor to help. People in the past have listened to my stories and constantly asked for more, or said they don't believe that one woman could do all these things, but this one did! Although I have changed a few names, and omitted a lot of details, this is my story, in a rough chronological order but chopped up into bite sized adventures and anecdotes.

Throughout my stories, it's clear that my boys aren't always with me. Sometimes I was away for days, but I would like to clarify that they were never left on their own.

Initially, I was lucky to have neighbours who would stay with them when I worked overnight. I had wonderful neighbours who helped me if I was working during school holidays or if I was late home. During my time in Turkey I had three different live-in nannies. I had an amazing friend with an internet café and a great Mum. The kids would play in the internet café, Huseyin would check what they were watching and playing. He would keep them safe and his Mum would make them food! Not the ideal thing to do, but when I was working in and around Alanya, either for Travel companies or when I was trying to get my little business enterprise started, I really, really had no option.

My Mum and Dad were great, and once they lived down the road, they would have the boys if I was away overnight. Looking back, I wonder if they must have thought I was on holiday, but I was working and it paid my rent. At one point I was working for someone on a sort of retainer, as they knew that if I was away from Alanya I couldn't make money repping or guiding.

I've had a truly weird, sometimes incredibly hard, sometimes sad, sometimes funny, sometimes very successful, but always amazing life. I made mistakes, I upset my boys with some of my decisions, but deep down most of what I did was to just get us all through life, with a roof over our heads, food in our bellies and bills paid. So when you read this, please don't judge me, just put yourself in my place and ask if you would have got through it!

I do not intend to upset, offend or bad mouth anyone. I want to entertain. You may not like or agree with some things I have done, or the way the book is written, but love it or hate it I hope it can make you smile at least a couple of times.

What follows is a collection of stories, anecdotes and adventures which make up the chaotic life of this fat bird!

Amça Bar, Bodrum

Way back in 1990 I was living with Nick. I'd met him in the supermarket where we both worked. We had been living together for a couple of years and the relationship was, well it was fairly bland. Our normal week consisted of working full time during the week, and on a Saturday night we would wander round to the local working men's club for a night out. Most of the people in the club worked at the same place, and for me it was sometimes like going to work, as I was employed in the personnel office. People would sometimes start asking me questions about their wages, or sick pay, or holidays. I helped them, but it was sometimes like working a shift.

As we knew almost everyone, Nick would wander around chatting to his mates, and invariably I would end up pretty much on my own with just an occasional chat. At the time it didn't occur to me that I should mind. I thought it was just normal and I didn't expect any more. Nick was also a gambler, and every day he was either planning his bets, or he was physically at the betting office. That was something I didn't deal with very well, and it caused more than a couple of arguments.

Over a Sunday lunch with Mum and Dad we all decided that a holiday together would be arranged. Within a few days I had booked a holiday for us all to Bodrum in Turkey. Nick and I had been to Turkey the previous year and we really liked it. All sorted for May.

May arrived and off we flew to Turkey, transferred to our hotel and our holiday began. Bodrum was a lovely place, with a harbour area that had restaurants and bars along the harbour side. There was a castle high on the hill which

1

looked down onto a busy bazaar area with some great shopping.

Each evening, for almost the whole of first week, we followed the same routine, being around the pool during the day, having a light lunch, followed by a shower, a change of clothing and a wander into town. We would have dinner and a couple of drinks, then wander back to the hotel. We were normally back in the hotel for 10.30pm! At the end of our first week, as we were walking back to the hotel, I was hanging back a little behind Mum and Dad. I motioned to Nick that we should stop for a drink at the bar we were just walking past. We told Mum and Dad, but they were ready to get back to the hotel, so we agreed to part there and see them in the morning. The bar was called the Amca Bar, pronounced Amja, and it means Uncle. The staff were fun, and we had a couple of good hours drinking and laughing.

The following night we did the same thing, but the problem was Nick really seemed to think we were back in our social club in the UK. Why? Well, the previous night we had met two couples, one was from York so from our 'neck of the woods', the second couple were from Kent. Now I'm not antisocial or stuck up, but the couple from York got on my nerves almost instantly! You know the type, you've been to Tenerife and they're been to Elevenerife! I found it hard to stick with their conversations and really didn't want to spend any further time with them! The couple from Kent? Well, they were so far up their own bottoms. They were outwardly well off, but boy they wanted everyone to know it. And for me…. Well that was enough of that as well!

The second night in the bar, we got drinks, and that was the night I was introduced to Turkish Vodka, it tastes very similar to Bacardi when mixed with cola. And then, as Nick was chatting with his new mates, I sat on my own watching the world go by as people walked past the bar. I didn't mind, even then, it had become normal and it was slightly better than answering questions about sick pay!

I think it was during our third night there that, once I was settled and left on my own, the waiter put a drink in front of me. He indicated that it had been bought by a friend of his who was sitting at the bar! I was a bit embarrassed, but looked to this guy and did my best to say thank you in a sort of pantomime way. When I thought it was safe to check him out, I saw that he was rather striking looking. Not good looking, but certainly not ugly. He had a chiselled jaw, and I mean it was square! Longish hair, not the thick 'waterproof' type Turkish hair, instead it seemed to be quite fine. He was sitting smoking at the end of the bar chatting with the bar staff. I was flattered, but thought no more about it. I told Nick as we walked back to the hotel and he just said 'Lucky you'.

The next night, once again I was on my own, once again people watching, and another drink arrived. This time it was held by the man with the chin made from marble! He couldn't speak English and I could only say thanks and please in Turkish so it was a little awkward, but I said thank you and beckoned him to sit down. I managed to give him my name and I managed to ascertain his was Erkan. I felt a little guilty trying to chat, as Nick was around the corner of the bar and couldn't see me. But we were doing nothing wrong. We had a little help from the waiter, Hassan, who had known Erkan for a long time. I was told he was a commercial scuba diver, and he had been going into the Amca Bar for a couple of years, but rarely drank alcohol as it was dangerous to drink and dive!

Nick appeared at one point, and I couldn't make my mind up if I was a little miffed, or if I was pleased he trusted me when he brightly asked if I needed another drink. When I said no I'd been bought one, he brightly skipped away to listen to Mr and Mrs Look-at-Me, and Mr and Mrs We-can-beat-that!

Erkan later explained that if he had thought that Nick and I were a 'couple' that he would never have bought me a drink, let alone approached me. I guess Nick and I were giving off 'just friends' signals.

Well, things sort of escalated over the next couple of days. Erkan sat with me for a time each evening, we tried to talk, we laughed at each other, and with the help of Hassan the waiter, we learned a little about each other. On the fourth night, with Hassan's help, Erkan asked me to go for a walk with him, he wanted to show me the boat he worked on. Mmmm yeah is that like showing me your etchings? But just as this question was asked, Nick appeared. I told him, and I really wanted him to say 'F*** off', but what he actually said told me that, whatever happened in my future, Nick would not feature in it. His reply was 'Yeah sure, just make sure you come back to me!' What the hell did that mean?

I think more out of spite than any other motive, I said yes to Erkan, and I walked out of the bar with him! I was so mad at Nick, so mad at myself, and basically thought sod it! But Erkan was as good as his word, and he unknowingly walked me back towards our hotel where a lot of the bigger commercial boats were moored. He showed me the only metal boat in the harbour, jumped on board and dug out a wet suit, grinning like a Cheshire cat. He clearly loved his job, whatever it was! I discovered later that he was part of a team of divers who were working to lay pipes, and it was a 3 year contract. He was diving much deeper than I think he should have been without specialist equipment, but he didn't seem to care.

After we had seen the boat, we found a wall and he took his coat off. I sat on his coat and we quite literally watched the sun come up. He then walked me back to the end of the road where my hotel was.

When I got into the hotel room Nick was there. He'd been sick and had climbed into bed leaving the bathroom in a shocking state. The next day, nothing, but nothing, was said of the previous night. I started to think it had been a dream! That evening, Mum and Dad picked up that something wasn't quite right, and when I said I wanted to go back to the hotel instead of calling in the Amca bar they pushed for the reason. I put it down to being tired. We walked really quickly past the bar!

I didn't think I'd done anything terribly wrong, as Nick clearly didn't care what I did or who with. He'd helped me make a decision about my future, and I think he knew it. He even asked me why I didn't want to see the 'boyfriend'. And I remember answering something like 'well clearly I should have'.

The following night was our last night in Bodrum, and I decided to go back to the bar, again more for spite than any other reason. I liked Erkan, but he was in a different country, he led a nomadic life, travelling where the work was. What could actually happen? I needed to explain to him my circumstances and that I was heading home so he didn't just think I'd vanished without a word.

That night, as I was sitting on my own, I had a visit from the female half of the couple from Kent, Mrs We-can-beat-that. She came to tell me off! She started telling me what a shit woman I was to leave Nick! I had very little to say to this woman, but I did advise her to wind her neck in and walk away before I showed her what I was really like! I felt bad enough but this was not something that I had created myself. I hadn't planned it, but to be honest I didn't really regret it. I felt flattered, I felt like a woman and I had enjoyed the time I spent with Erkan.

Erkan joined me, and this time it was me that asked him to go for a walk. I wanted him to slowly walk me back to the hotel. Before he did, he steered me down towards the lighthouse on the harbour and we sat down. He was trying to ask me something and it took me ages to understand, until I realised he was asking when I was leaving Turkey. I told him, and I could see he was disappointed, and to be fair so was I. He asked for my phone number. These were the days before mobiles and I lived with Nick! But I gave him the number. I truly never thought he'd use it. He had no number to give me but was constantly saying Hassan, Amca Bar, so I guessed he was saying he would use the phone in the bar! And I was guessing he planned for Hassan to help him. But that sounded like a lot of hard work, so again I didn't dwell on it.

He walked me to the road where the hotel was, and I let him walk a little of the way up to the hotel. When it was time to leave him, we kissed for the first time and had a hug. I turned to go. After a couple of metres, I turned to watch the marble chin stranger go, just in time to see him thump the wall he was walking past really hard!

We flew back to the UK the following day. I hardly said a word to anyone, and wasn't sure if I was glad to be home or not!

Oh My Goodness!

My first call from Erkan and Hassan was two days after I arrived home, late in the evening. I was absolutely stunned. Nick and I had already fallen apart but I had no intention of making things any worse than they were already. We would be splitting up, no doubt about it, but did I want to continue talking to Erkan? Well yes, I did and we talked at least once every week, but sometimes as many as 3 or 4 times. The telephone at home was in a different room from where the TV was, so I had privacy and didn't embarrass or upset Nick. He had quickly realised that the things he'd done and said, and the things he should have done and should have said but never did, had helped to bring us to this moment. I took my share of responsibility, but there must have been a major problem before we went away for this to even happen. We decided to make a clean break, it was time. He was happy to take the mortgage on the house over, and I was happy with that. I would take out anything personal and he could keep the rest. He could have the dog, as I had nowhere to take him if I moved back with Mum and Dad, which is what I ultimately did.

Fortunately for me, as I know I would have received a lot of grief from the staff in the supermarket, I applied for, and was offered, a new job. That meant new people who didn't know anything about my history or my 'shameful' holiday. I quickly settled in with them, and I moved back in with Mum and Dad. They were shocked, but as ever, supportive. Whatever happened now, I had made a new start, a new life. I loved my new job, which was working for a company who were finding work for the unemployed of a local village. The people were great and I had no history, so I was happy.

9

It was about the end of June when I got a letter from Erkan. Written, I guessed, by Hassan, but the sentiments were Erkan's. He asked me to go out to Turkey and spend a week with him. I had holidays accrued so I decided August would be a good time and I booked the week. I booked the flight into Dalaman, but I had also spotted hotels and had recorded numbers for transfers in case things went wrong. I was taking a massive chance after all.

When I arrived at Manchester airport there were delays to almost every flight going to Turkey, and during the wait I made friends with three other girls, who it turned out were all going out to Turkey to see guys they had met on holiday. They were great girls, and they gave me the names of their hotels in case I came unstuck! We laughed, we got slightly drunk and we talked about each other's romances and how we had met. We slept on the flight, but I was worried since Erkan had said he would meet me at the airport, and we were late. The other girls had planned to use a taxi together, but had been kind enough to say they would check that I was OK before they left the airport, just in case I needed a lift.

I did discover a while later that the reason we were delayed was that the 20th Tactical Fighter Wing of the USAF were being deployed to Incirlik in Turkey for weapons training. This was when Iraq invaded Kuwait!

If you read to the end of this book, you'll spot a recurring theme with my life; War, Terrorism and more war. You couldn't make this up.

When we arrived at Dalaman I could barely breath, but as I walked out of the terminal building I saw a familiar jacket walking up the ramp from the car park, and then that chiselled chin with a smiley face! Phew! The girls saw us hugging, they cheered and walked off.

Erkan put me in a taxi and we headed off. He had clearly been learning English and I had been trying to learn a little more Turkish. Strangely enough, and Mum, Dad and later on Erkan's family, could never understand it, we developed our own language. It wasn't English and it wasn't Turkish, it was an odd mix just for us. But it worked well until we both learned each other's language properly.

We arrived at a hotel in Bodrum. It was very odd, the pool was empty, the garden looked unkempt and there was absolutely no one there. Erkan, through his little bit of English, my understanding of a little Turkish, a little red dictionary and pantomime, explained that the hotel was owned by a friend who had let us stay there. He unlocked a room. Wonderful, it was complete! The furniture was all there, clean and tidy, the bed made beautifully, the bathroom was clean and tidy with big white fluffy towels. It was everything I could have hoped for.

We spent the days in Bodrum with Erkan showing me around. He introduced me to real Turkish food, we walked along the harbour each evening, and we even surprised Hassan by turning up together in the Amca bar. We had a wonderful week together. I saw the behind the scenes Bodrum, and I fell in love with seeing things that tourists rarely get to see.

I left Turkey with a very heavy heart, especially as I had discovered the previous evening that Erkan had lost his diving job because he had asked for a week off. In 18 months, he had never taken a day's holiday. Now he wasn't being allowed to, so he had walked off. When he dropped me back at the airport he planned to go collect his belongings and head back home to Izmir until he found employment. Before I left, we had discussed when I would go back to Turkey again. October seemed like the best plan. I would have holidays to take again by then, and money. Once I was home, Erkan and I continued to speak every day, but this time it was me ringing him at his Mum's home. I would stand at the bottom of the stairs and my Mum and Dad would sit watching TV as we spoke. We had really moved forward with our own language, they could rarely understand anything we said.

The Next Small Step

During one of our evening phone conversations, Erkan told me that he wanted me to visit Izmir at some point during my next visit, to meet his family. We were moving into scary waters here.

I had rekindled a friendship with a girl I had spent my 'nightclubbing years' with before this trip to Izmir had been introduced into the agenda. She had said that she would love to come out to Turkey with me. She was great fun and was happy to stay behind the scenes and do her own thing when Erkan and I wanted time alone. I was a bit dubious at first, but then thought sure, why not? I was, I guess, still worried that things might go wrong and I'd be stuck out there on my own.

Now that the trip to Izmir had been brought up, I really didn't want to tell her what I was planning. I asked my Mum and Dad's advice as to what I should do. To my great surprise, my Mum, who really wasn't that adventurous, or so I thought, suggested that she should come out to Turkey with me and Karen. She would stay with Karen and keep her company during the days I went to Izmir. Deal done. Karen was OK with it all, so we booked to fly into Dalaman.

We landed in Dalaman, and since we had booked a package holiday, we took up the transfer into Bodrum, which took about 90 minutes. I had arranged to meet Erkan once we arrived in town. To make it easy for Erkan, we arranged to meet at the Amca Bar.

We booked into the hotel, unpacked and had a quick drink. I think we were all nervous by then, and I often wonder what Erkan was feeling like. The time came to meet and we left a little early, took a taxi into town and walked into the Amca Bar. It was the middle of the afternoon and it was baking hot, so we sat inside. Erkan appeared within a couple of minutes and we all kissed, hugged and introduced each other. Erkan then asked, in his newly refined English, what we wanted to drink, and once orders were taken, he headed off to the bar. Mum and Karen were all ooo's and ahhhhh's as to how polite he was and how odd his chin was!

The next few minutes somehow clicked into slow motion, or at least they did in my head. As Erkan left the bar, Hassan handed him a glass of tea. Now if you've been to Turkey you'll know that tea is served in a little tulip shaped glass on a saucer with a tiny spoon and normally a lot of sugar. Now imagine this. Between the bar area and the indoor seating area where we were, there were two different types of flooring, and so a small step. When I say small, I mean less than a centimetre. But these tiny steps can be tricky little bastards. We have all probably tripped over one in our lifetime, haven't we?

Well, as Erkan was walking back towards us, and I know he must have been so nervous, the toe of his boot caught the step. Erkan then launched forward trying incredibly hard to both look cool and keep his balance. The glass with the tea wobbled quite badly on the saucer, making a lovely chinking noise. Mum, Karen and I gasped. I'm laughing as I type this, I can still see Erkan stumble, but in his defence, he stayed upright, lost only half of his tea into the saucer and only turned a little pink, rather than deep red. It, if you pardon the pun, broke the ice and we all got on like a house on fire after that.

We spent a couple of days together, a night out at a wonderful Turkish restaurant, and everyone had a good time. That evening Erkan said we would be heading to Izmir the following day, and so we did. We climbed onto a coach and several hours later we climbed off in Izmir. I did go to Izmir quite often after that first visit, but that first time it was scary, busy and all foreign, nothing like the holiday resorts I had been to previously. The further away from the bus station we went, the narrower the streets became. We finally stopped in front of a tiny little house with 3 steps to get down to the front door. Erkan's Mum came flying out and grabbed me like I was a long lost family member. She was lovely, always was. And then to my incredible relief, Erkan's younger brother appeared, and he spoke English.

We spent two days in Izmir, I was scared, out of my depth with the language, intrigued and happy all at the same time. Scared as I really had no idea how to get back to Dalaman airport, I doubt very much if I could have even found my way out of the small narrow roads. Well, not without wandering for hours. And to get to the bus station in the middle of Izmir? I was scared. I was seriously struggling, but Erkan's brother, Ertan, was a star. He was a funny guy who had spent a few years in hotel receptions, so his English was good enough to help me out, and to help me answer the thousand questions as the family asked them.

One morning, we got up, had breakfast and headed out. Ertan explained we were going to meet family. Now if someone had said that to you, what would you think? A couple of people, another family, so maybe Mum, Dad and kids? Ha! Not in this case. We arrived at a house about a 15 minute steady walk away. Erkan, his Mum, his brother Ertan, and I. Plus Erkan's Dad, who I was only lucky enough to meet a couple of times. He was quite a character, he loved his Raki and would sit telling me lots of tales. The fact that I couldn't understand him seemed irrelevant, but I loved sitting with him and watching him become so animated.

We all took our shoes off and walked into the house we were visiting. I have never seen so many people packed into such a small space! It seemed that I was quite an attraction. I suppose, when I think back it was 1990, and although it happens a lot now, way back then, there weren't many English or Foreigners in Turkey wandering around places where tourists rarely went. I discovered that day that many of the people we were visiting had never met a foreigner before. A couple of years later, whilst visiting Erkan's Mum with our eldest son as an 11 week old baby, we visited the same house, with all the same people. That day they were amazed that I had my son in an outfit with big brightly coloured spots on it. They thought he should have been swaddled and with his head covered. Bear in mind we were inside a house, it was crowded and very hot, so Nooo, Aslan loved the sun and didn't like to be covered. He was kicking and waving his hands all over as if he was conducting the madness going on around him that day.

Anyway, after a couple of days in Izmir, we took the coach back to Bodrum and had another couple of days together. Mum and Karen hadn't killed each other, and had enjoyed their days. Erkan and I were getting on fantastically, and it seemed that I had passed the meet-the-family test, and so had he.

During that time, Erkan asked me to marry him. Bear in mind that, although I had known him a year, I had only spent time with him for a few days in total. I didn't say no, but I didn't say yes either. It was quick, and I did wonder if he just wanted a visa to come to the UK. Everyone I talked to said the same thing, and I didn't have enough confidence to be 100% sure of myself.

The Families Meet

I was really mixed up, not quite sure what to think or believe. But life trickled along and it was heading to Christmas. Once again, I was invited back to Turkey and this time Mum and Dad were invited too. Dad was surprised, but gratefully accepted. Again flights were booked, this time to Izmir. As Christmas approached, I started looking at what was needed to get Erkan to come to the UK, how difficult it might be, was it even possible? It seemed possible, it was mainly a check that he had enough funds to support himself when he got to the UK, or had someone who could prove they could support him. I had a good job, and after discussing it with Mum and Dad, they said they were OK with him moving in until we found accommodation. They were happy to write a letter for the Consulate if it helped. I made a decision and booked an appointment for mid-January at the British Consulate in Istanbul to apply for a visa for Erkan to be allowed into the UK. The worst that could happen was they would refuse, or that he got here, turned into a pleb and we split up. But if we weren't together then it was the government he would have to talk to about his visa and staying in England.

We all flew out to Turkey just before Christmas. We were armed with presents and food and souvenirs from England. We had a brand new pushchair for Erkan's eldest brother, Ercan, and his wife who had just had a baby girl. I had noticed that pushchairs in Turkey were very basic, and we had been told that we were all staying at Ercan's home. Erkan said they wouldn't take any money from us for food etc, so we thought a modern pushchair would be a good way to say thanks. We were welcomed with open arms, and they loved the pushchair and appreciated the thought.

Erkan later told me that the pushchair caused a real stir, and neighbours and friends were seriously jealous.

Mum and Dad, and Erkan's Mum and Dad, chatted to each other as best they could. We would all eat together, and one evening Mum and I volunteered to shop for, then cook, an English meal. We made a roast dinner with chops and it was enjoyed by everyone.

Christmas wasn't celebrated for obvious reasons, but once Christmas had been and gone, everyone in Izmir started to put out their trimmings and Christmas Trees. We were asked if we wanted to go window shopping so we all tripped out on New Year's Eve during the afternoon. One of Erkan's cousins came with us., A nice girl who could speak English, which was a great help again. We all thought that we were slightly mental that day. We had never been in such a busy place as the bazaar area. Imagine, if you can, the busiest Christmas Eve ever, combined with a Black Friday run on a shop almost giving stock away and then multiply that by ten. That was what we walked into. Mum was terrified, Dad wandered about whistling and smiling, I was hanging onto my handbag as I was convinced someone would steal it, and Erkan was running about trying to shepherd us all. I mention this only because that day seemed to confirm to everyone that Erkan was a truly nice guy, we all arrived home safe and with handbags, purses and wallets intact!

We all spent New Year's Eve together and we left for the UK on 2nd January 1991. That was a hard day full of tears from everyone. I think I cried most of the way home, but I did know that I would be going back in a few short weeks which eased the hurt a little.

The First Visa, The First War

Stick with the book and you will understand the title, but here we are, I'm sitting watching the late news on the TV at Mum and Dad's house the night before I am due to fly off to Istanbul to apply for Erkan's visa to come to the UK. It was mid-January 1990, and just before I turned the TV off to head for bed, a news flash appeared telling everyone that Operation Desert Storm had just commenced, in the defence of Kuwait. I went to bed not really knowing if I would still be flying to Turkey the following day.

I got up, and the first thing to do was to call the airline. They confirmed that flights were still going to Istanbul. Had I chosen to cancel then I would have lost the cost of my ticket, so I set off. I'd spoken to my boss to advise him I was still flying out there, and that I'd let him know what was happening when I could. Remember, we didn't have mobiles back then. I couldn't call Erkan as he would have already jumped on a bus to get up to Istanbul to meet me, and he would have done that at the time I was watching the crappy news. So I had to have faith that he would be there.

I was incredibly nervous when I got off the plane in Istanbul. I was, way back then, still a relative novice at flying, particularly on my own. But I was also worried that I would walk out of the terminal building and be on my own. A thousand questions formed. How would I get hold of Erkan if he wasn't there? Where on earth would I go? I had brought more money with me than I hoped we'd need, the days of good old traveller's cheques. I'd ordered them, queued for a while in the travel agent's and stood forever signing every one of them. I wasn't worried about getting a hotel, I could do that, but I had come out on a one-way ticket as the plan was to get his visa and then buy two one-way tickets to get home. Everything had been a worry back when we were planning it, but now more than ever. Everything had fallen to pieces the previous night.

However, these were the 'Good Erkan' days and he was diligently waiting for me at the arrivals gate. We were both worried, but there was absolutely nothing we could do to change what had been set in motion. We found the British Consulate General building, and booked into a nearby hotel for the night. We were hoping that we wouldn't be staying in Istanbul for very long. We didn't sleep well, the next day was to be a turning point in our lives, one way or another. If we didn't get the visa, Erkan had asked if I would move to Turkey, and I was seriously considering it!

The following day we were up and ready early, breakfast wouldn't work. We both sat in the restaurant of the hotel and all we could face was coffee. We asked the hotel to put our baggage in storage for a few hours. I had taken the minimum of things and Erkan really didn't have that much, but it was all he owned.

We walked across to the Consulate, and the first thing we saw was an armed guard standing a couple of metres away from the main gate used for visa applications. There hadn't been an armed guard there the day before. This was alarming as I couldn't get near to any English speaker. There was a queue forming, people like ourselves wanting visa's, mostly solo men. There was one couple, way back in the queue, but they were both Turkish. Everyone was questioning each other, but clearly none of us had an answer. At some point during the morning, a notice was fastened up stating that the Consulate had closed due to the potential threat of terrorism!

What on earth would we all do? Strangely we all stood and continued to queue. I think we were all stunned and disappointed, these appointments were all incredibly important life changing moments in life. But we were lucky and were very near the front of the queue. I saw a young woman walk through the gate and out onto the road. I dashed after her, apologising and explaining our situation. She was extremely kind and took the time to explain that the consulate had been closed because it was almost impossible to tell the difference between an Iraqi and a Turk, so until they could make the process safe for staff they were closing it.

She asked where we had travelled from and I explained, I had flown in, but Erkan lived in Izmir. She said all she could advise was to wait a few days as things might change quickly, and that she thought they would be reopening at some point soon.

Erkan and I left the queue and went for a drink. We sat with two teas going cold in front of us and no plan. Did we hang about in Istanbul? If we did, we needed to move to a cheaper place as the hotels near the Consulate weren't the cheapest. Did we head back to Izmir which was probably 8 hours or more on the coach but at least we weren't paying for hotels? The coaches were relatively cheap and are a comfortable way to move about in Turkey.

We decided that, as we didn't know how long this would go on for, we would head to Izmir. We collected our luggage and headed to the bus station. We travelled through the night for about 8 and a bit hours, and arrived in Izmir very tired and deflated. Erkan had hoped that he wouldn't see his family again so quickly, and they too were deflated and disappointed for us. They welcomed us back and made breakfast for us. It had been a long 24 hours.

Now I'm not sure of the timings here, but I was well into my cheese, tomato and fresh bread breakfast when the phone rang.

Erkan's mum answered and told Erkan the call was for him. He took the handpiece from his Mum and spoke to the caller. I didn't take a lot of notice as I was trying to have a conversation with Erkan's Dad. But then Erkan put the phone down and told me the news. I didn't know whether to laugh or cry. It was the Consulate and they were calling to say they were reopening, and did we want an appointment the following day? Erkan had said yes of course. After breakfast and a shower we were off back to the bus station…

Little bit of déjà vu but another 8 and a bit hours later we were stepping off another coach, back where we had started. We were so tired but we had a full night before our appointment the next day so headed back to the same hotel we had stayed in previously. It felt like weeks had passed, but it was just a couple of days. We both slept like the dead that night.

The following day, off we went. Same routine, a queue outside the gate, armed guards everywhere, but this time the queue was moving forwards. Once we were at the front, we were escorted through the gate and a large turnstile on the other side, through an office and through the similar sort of security you would expect to find in an airport. We were then seated in a corridor until a woman appeared and shouted Erkan's name. We went into a large room with desks down one side, with new screens in front of them. We were later told that the screens were bullet proof and had just been installed so that the visa section could re-open.

We were seated in front of two women. One was the Consulate staff member and the other her Turkish translator. Now, I don't know who was looking after us that day, but it turned out that the translator was from Izmir, so she and Erkan had an instant bond. The Consulate staff member had been sitting on the plane in the row in front of me when Mum, Dad and I flew back after our Christmas visit. She told me she remembered seeing how upset I was. She had also seen Mum and Dad with me, which added kudos to our application, apparently.

Questions were asked, and the lovely translator from Izmir sometimes translated Erkan's reply slightly differently to his actual reply. Erkan told me later that she was helping. I had a folder of paperwork, including payslips and Mum and Dad's letter saying Erkan would have a home in the UK. A local councillor had also given Mum and Dad a reference at my request, and that backed Mum and Dad up. I had included bank details and a little folder I'd put together explaining how and where we would be trying to ensure Erkan found employment quickly. I had several personal references, and was very well prepared if I say so myself! I had figured out through reading up and researching that we really only had only one shot, and with the expenses of the visa, we were going to get it as good as we could first time. Payment for the visa was taken whether it was issued or not.

Following our interview, the words, 'I'm pleased to say you have been successful in your application' were some of the best words I had ever heard. We were asked to wait a short while, and about 15 minutes later the Consulate staff member came out and gave Erkan his passport back. Inside it was a full page visa granting him entry to the UK. We were on the road to a life together. We weren't finished regarding visa's if my memory serves me well. We needed to apply for anther visa once Erkan arrived in the UK, as the one in his passport didn't allow him to work. The second visa would grant permission to work and to get married, and that would last for three years. If we were married and settled, then we could apply for an indefinite leave to remain visa, and once he'd had that in his passport for some time, then he could apply for British Citizenship. I had no qualms about any of this, as we intended to work hard and not be a burden on anyone, particularly the British government, and I'm pleased to say we never were.

We left the Consulate in a fabulous mood, we sat and ate the first proper meal we had eaten in about four days, and although part of the world close by was at war, we relaxed. But only for a couple of hours.

Out next mission was to find and buy a flight home. The internet was still new back then and so that wasn't an option. We went back to the hotel, booked in for another night and I got to work on the phone. And when I say I got to work, I mean I called company after company. I was told that most of them had cancelled their flights for the short term, and the ones that were still flying were full. Oh my God, another decision as to what to do? We decided this time to move to a much cheaper hotel. Once checked in there, I phoned my Mum and my boss. Mum was thrilled we had 'our' Visa. Boss was thrilled we had the visa, but not overly impressed when I told him I didn't know when I would be back! But he knew I had no choice so told me to 'do my best'.

I did my best, and three days later we boarded a plane bound for the UK. We were still nervous and although we had done everything properly, and had all the correct paperwork and Visa's, we assumed that Erkan could still be refused entry, even at that point. We queued, we were checked, and we were in!

The Early Years

Our first few years in the UK were good years. We lived with Mum and Dad for the first few months, Erkan helped out wherever he could. He painted everything that didn't move, he helped Mum in the garden. We had found him a Turkish/English translator so he was trying his best to learn more English.

We married at the local registry office in March, a low key affair with Mum and Dad, my brother and his family, a couple of friends and the people I worked with, who had been great throughout the whole thing. Erkan's translator was his best man. It was a nice wedding, followed by a small party at a local pub. We had a beautifully made cake and a small buffet. It was a lovely day.

We were now in a position to apply for a visa for Erkan that would enable us to find him a job. This was fairly straight forward, and once his passport was back in his hand with his new visa in, we started looking for a job for him.

There were a few false starts, with job offers that turned out to not be what was promised. We had invested in a small motorbike for Erkan, as without transport there would have been little chance. We lived in a rural area which had been a mining village, both when we lived with Mum and Dad and even when we found a house we could afford to move into. This was still miles from most work.

Whilst still with Mum and Dad, Erkan started work with a Powder coating company. Powder coating is a very dirty job, it's basically spraying powder onto metal furniture that is then run through an over and the powder sets to make a hard lasting coat. That's an easy explanation, but trust me, it's a filthy, thankless job. Erkan travelled in daily, and rarely moaned, he was just happy to be earning. The sad thing was that, during a call to his Mum, he told her how much he was earning. He was thrilled to bits with it. I was happy that he was working, but knew his wages by English standards were very poor. However, his family thought he was a rich man. From that first phone call right to the end, every time we visited Turkey they would ask us for a list of things a mile long. We would take some things, and then we would need to explain over and over that things like a packet of cigarettes probably cost 10 times as much in the UK than they did in Turkey, so his wages really were not that high.

I was saddened, because this meant he started spacing the calls to his Mum out, and I knew it was because he was growing tired of explaining about his money all the time.

He settled into the UK way of doing things, and although he was working with a few guys who were seriously rough, they were also working. On one particular day, Erkan came home from work and was sitting looking at his little red book which was a Turkish/English dictionary. This little red book had been used so much in the past year or so and did look tatty, but it worked. He seemed to be struggling, the spelling of some of the English words were particularly difficult, as the Turkish spelling was for me. I asked if I could help. He explained that he had heard a word a lot, the other guys in the factory were always saying it, and they called each other it all the time. OK says I what was it?

'C**t!' One of the words I hate most in the English language. I remember my reply was ' errr I don't think you'll find that in there' and then I went on to explain the word, and how it was normally used.

Because we were now working we managed to secure a mortgage for a great little house. I'd taken a temporary promotion at work which was a step up, to being an advisor, rather than a receptionist. I had my own office in another mining town a few miles away from Mum and Dad. The move made things a little difficult for Erkan, as it meant a really long bike ride to work. But then we managed to get him a job in another Powder coating company nearer our new home.

The birth of my boys is explained in a separate 'story', but we were doing OK. Erkan changed jobs again, and I must say I could help a lot with his jobs, as I was lucky enough to be in the right place. My job was finding jobs for people. He started working for a big company that managed the warehousing for a large supermarket chain. He stayed there until we left the UK.

During this time I probably couldn't have asked for a better husband. He started working nights as it was a lot more money and he would arrive home on a morning. In the winter, he would go warm the car up before I put the boys in to take them to Mum's. He helped with housework, he changed nappies and helped me with the boys. We only went out when all bills were paid and we had spare cash. Even then we went out as a family, to the coast or sometimes a kids' theme park.

We had always talked about moving back to Turkey one day and we were saving up, easier now that Erkan had his new job. Then life takes its turns to slow you down. I was pregnant for the second time. I was happy to be pregnant, I had been told years before that it was unlikely that I would ever be able to have kids. Then, part way through my pregnancy, I was made redundant.

Not one to get stuck, I had my second son and approached a friend who I had worked with, but who had been offered a better job and left. She was doing a similar job for a different company now, and I asked if there were any jobs going there. There were, I was once again lucky, and I started there when my youngest was a tiny baby.

Mum and Dad had the boys for me whilst I worked, and we continued saving. We visited Turkey as often as we could. Erkan was unable to travel very far, even on holidays as his visa was always a problem for the first years, so we tried to have two trips back to Turkey, one in a resort as a family holiday, sometimes even with Mum and Dad coming with us, and one to visit his Mum. His Dad had unfortunately passed away shortly after our first visit with our eldest son.

We lived like this for several years, I climbed jobs with my company until I was running several sections, and I absolutely loved what I was doing. I was good at it too, so bonuses were plentiful and money was hitting the bank now. Life took another turn again, and the government changed the way it was funding companies like ourselves and we lost our contract. I was once again out of work, but then I was head-hunted by yet another company who had benefitted from our loss of contract.

I started there without a gap in my employment, but I didn't like it. I was a little out of my comfort zone running job seekers clubs, as I wanted to be proactive and get these guys back to work, not sit in a classroom.

Erkan and I had already met someone during the last holiday we took, in a place called Alanya. Murat and his father owned a building company and were looking for partners/investors in a holiday hotel that they had built. Erkan and I were seriously considering his offer.

I had changed my job again, but I wasn't enjoying it. So we made the monumental decision that the time was right and it was time to go. The boys were at an age where they would be OK. Aslan, the eldest, was 6, and Kaan, the youngest, was 3. They were no longer babies, and I could cope. We spoke to Murat for hours, sorted finances and agreed that we could move into the empty but finished hotel when we arrived in Turkey, and start from there. It was finally time to go.

My Boys

My wonderful boys were born in the UK in Yorkshire. My eldest, Aslan, was due on his Dad's birthday but arrived 10 days early. I was perhaps responsible for that as I was in hospital on bed rest during a particulary hot summer. From my week long stay, I only remember a few things. One was a special lady called Sue who was in there for being vulnerable to pre-eclampsia. We ended up being split up and put onto different bays in the ward because we would make each other laugh all the time. Seeing her with her ma-ooo-sive bra on her head like a pilots helmet, well that one will stay with me forever. During this time pregnancy lock-down, the hospital had started to clean the front of the hospital by sand blasting it. So, every morning, very early, the noise of the guys outside fitting and moving all the scaffolding was how I started my day. Once the scaffolding was in place, the sand blasting would begin, the noise was one thing, having to have all the windows closed in that heat was another!

Strangely enough, my consultant was an odd man, as most consultants, in my opinion seem to be, everyone was scared of him! But he lived in the 'old part' of the same village my Mum lived in, and she was employed as his cleaner. He knew I was her daughter, so he was OK with me, and during out-patient visits I had discovered he did actually have a sense of humour. One particularly hot, sticky and noisy day however, I'd had enough! My consultant stood at the bottom of my bed checking my charts, with two midwives standing behind him. I won't use his correct name so let's just call him Dr Strangelove. 'Dr Strangelove,' I ask, 'Where do you park your car?' As I spoke, I saw the look of fear on the midwives faces. Apparently you're not supposed to speak to the consultants like they have lives, or that they are real people! Ha! Dr Strangelove, looked up from the charts and over the top of his glasses. He was attempting to wear a small grin, but it somehow didn't fit his face! He answered, 'Why'? Well, Dr Strangelove, if you don't start me off into labour, I plan to escape and waddle round and fire bomb your car! He grinned broadly, the midwives glared at me, shaking their heads and looking positively scared to death, and I though mmm maybe that was a bit much, but any of you that have given birth will know exactly how I was thinking.

A serious conversation then followed between Dr Strangelove and myself, so he basically knew how I felt and agreed to start me off with the baby.

My beautiful, gorgeous son, Aslan, was born many, many hours later, by cesarian section. A memory that sticks with me was one of the two midwives coming into my room. I had, as I guess a lot of ladies do with a first baby, prepared a birth plan: no painkillers, no cutting blah blah blah. But she came in and I had weirdly turned into Thomas the Tank Engine and was sitting panting and puffing. 'You OK' she said. 'Nooooo!' I said, 'cut me open, just get this baby out!' She laughed and said something like 'Karma is a Bitch' as she walked off chuckling!

My second son, Kaan, was born on his fathers birthday. Erkan had gone to work, he worked nights and I went into labour naturally, but once at the hospital I received the upsetting news that another Cesarian was needed. However, my second beautiful son Kaan was born early Saturday morning and made my family complete.

I know we all believe our kids are THE best, and I'm no different. Two beautiful, slightly tanned looking boys. Healthy, large amounts of very dark thick hair, wonderful smiles and just perfection in a small bundle.

I've decided to use their real names, as much as they will be embarrassed, I love their names as much as I love them!

I'll share a few anecdotes relating to my wonderful boys in a few chapters later on.

Heading To Turkey And My Life Changes

Throughout my marriage to Erkan, our aim was always to head to Turkey, rent a hotel and live our lives out there. I was lucky, when we married all I had to do to obtain a Turkish Passport was to apply within 28 days of getting married, which I did. So I have had a Turkish Passport and a Kimlik (ID card) since 1991. I was very proud to have it, as I lived like a Turk as much as I could. I even voted once during my life there. I had decided to live my life out there and I wanted to be part of the country, not an ex-pat wanting to change everything to the European way!

One sunny day in November 1998 we stepped onto the minibus after saying a very tearful Goodbye to my parents. The minibus was packed with the four of us; Erkan, the two boys and myself, plus a pushchair, all the cases we thought we could carry, and a small holdall with 'can't leave behind' items.

I don't really want to dwell on the first few weeks of our move to Turkey. We had previously sent a considerable amount of money to our business partners in Turkey, for the rent of the hotel we had seen and signed contracts for, during a trip to Alanya a few months prior to moving out there. The plan was to live in one of the empty rooms in the hotel until we could get on our feet and find an affordable apartment. That was do-able as the rooms were designed to be self-catering, so we were pretty comfortable, we bought a small TV and a video player, and we were good.

The hotel was set up with contracts, one for the summer season with a Swedish company and then one with Saga for older people who wanted to go out to Turkey in the Autumn and we were set to have a busy year.

We had the best Christmas for the boys that we could. As Erkan was Muslim, and as the boys were being brought up as Muslims, we had always celebrated Christmas with Santa/Father Christmas, rather than with the religious side of things. We had brought our tree out with us, a pretty tree with fibre optic lights, so we didn't need any trimmings. We had brought presents out with us, so we did our best, but no grandparents, carol singing or Christmas parties, and no traditional dinner.

We got through the New Year but shortly afterwards Abdullah Ocalan the leader of the Kurdish PKK in Turkey was captured, and that pretty much put paid to any plans we had made. The Kurds threatened to start a bombing campaign in all the tourists resorts in Turkey. There had already been bombs left in litter bins and grenades thrown about, so it was no empty threat. The holiday companies started to cancel, and they cancelled in droves. Hardly anyone in Turkey had a contract or expected many guests.

We had found, and moved into, a small apartment. We tried our best to furnish it, and we had spent a little on the kitchen, toilet and bathroom as it was really, really in a mess.

I made friends. I'd found a group of ex-pat ladies who eventually formed a group. We were all in the same boat, some of us had small children, some were older ladies who had lived in Turkey long enough to know their way around and share information and advise the newbies.

We lived on the small amount of cash we had brought with us, and that wasn't much. I did my best to make economic meals, and I was trying to find any work that an English woman who spoke very little Turkish could do. A dear friend put me onto doing airport transfers, it wasn't a lot of money but it was a start. When I told Erkan, surprisingly he said that it would be better for him to apply so I could stay at home with the boys, as it was an overnight job. His English was good enough so I agreed. He did one transfer and when he explained how it had gone the following day, he said he would never do another, it was not enough money!

We were running out of money, since the hotel wouldn't open for months, if indeed it would open at all. The boys were attending a private school which we couldn't afford. We had been unable to send them to a government school as they didn't speak enough language to get by.

During those months Erkan started gambling, he was spending a lot of time with the builder of the hotel that we had gone into business with, and they were drinking heavily. Erkan, was never a big drinker, when he lived in Turkey he was a diver so couldn't drink, when we moved to the UK and had the boys, he rarely drank as we only went out sociably for special occasions or as a family.

Money became tighter than ever, arguments became more and more frequent, and for the first time in my life, I was struck by a man, my husband, the father of my kids. It came during an argument where I accused Erkan of doing nothing to make our horrible, horrible situation any better. He spoke really good English, we had lived in the UK for 8 years, he could fix anything mechanical, he knew so many things. Yet, instead of making use of his skills, he was drinking and secretly gambling.

During the argument, years ago I might have said I went too far! But I didn't. There's nothing I said, or could have said, that can make it OK for a man to hit a woman.

I was stunned, and I think he was. I stepped back, went into my bedroom and closed the door. My life had changed, and the change was irreversible.

Speaking Turkish

Now bear in mind people, that I'm talking about a time when Turkey wasn't what it is now. Tourists had only just found it in large numbers, so there was a lot of things that were still not up to 'European standards' One of these things were children's parks. Now, I was a child in the sixties and seventies, so I grew up with unsafe parks; rusty swings with dodgy chains, weird conical things that you could sit on and be swung around until you were sick. Roundabouts that, with the right 'pusher' were dangerous to be on as you couldn't get off, unless you were prepared to fall over and roll like a paratrooper on crack!

Anyway I digress.. again… Next to the very first apartment I lived in with the boys was one of these parks. It was extremely sandy in the summer, the floor baked as hard as concrete but in the winter the floor would turn into very deep very, very thick mud!

When the rains started at the end of the summer, Aslan had some good boots to deal with the mud and Kaan had a pair of bright red wellies that had been Aslan's and had come out to Turkey with us. Kaan loved these Wellies, like kids do, they never want to take certain things off, or they become obsessed with them, then suddenly and for no reason they go off things. Well Kaan was obsessed with his wellies, they were a little big, but he was happy to have a couple of pairs of socks. He would skip down the stairs in the apartment block. Each day, when it was time to get the boys indoors, was the same routine. They would get to the doorway of our apartment and I would have to strip them both off. They would be covered, and I mean absolutely covered in mud, from head to toe. They were having such a good time down in the park, how could I stop them! I marched them both down to the shower in their keks and they would shower the mud off as I stuffed the washer and cleared

41

up the mud. The washing machine was the best thing I owned at that time, old and noisy, but worth its weight in gold!

One particular day, I shouted the boys in. Aslan appeared at the door first, stripped, sent on his way to the shower, but no sign of Kaan. I shouted down the stairwell and heard some unintelligible grunt. A minute or two later Kaan appeared, but to my absolute horror he was covered in blood! I quickly scooped him up and took him into the kitchen, I didn't know where the blood was coming from, it took me more time than I wished to track it down to the bridge of his nose. It was absolutely gushing. Kaan was calm, not crying, just concerned as he only had one Wellington boot on! It took a while to stem the bleeding, I cleaned his wound up and cleaned his face. He explained that because he didn't have both Wellies on, he had tripped coming up the stairs and fallen. He had hit the bridge of his nose right across the corner of the step, they were marble steps! I'm cringing as I write this! He was OK, he didn't need medical attention once I'd traced his injury and cleaned him up. After his shower I was able to tape him up. He does still have a scar across the bridge of his nose, though.

The laughable thing about this is that, after I'd got them both sorted and sitting watching TV, I found myself outside. It was now raining, and I was in a pair of flip flops looking for Kaan's Wellington! I didn't own boots then, and I really didn't want to ruin any of my precious footwear. I did find the boot, I did clean it up and clean myself up. Kaan never knew. His precious boot lived on and I eventually had to cut the toes out of those boots so that he could wear them even when it was hot weather! Then one day he woke up and threw them in the bin! Kids hey!

We moved into this apartment during the school holidays and to be honest it was a godsend as not having any language and with my marriage to the boys' Dad being not so good now, it was a good way of letting the boys out to make friends and get used to their new surroundings. If I sat on the balcony of my apartment I could watch them, without them really knowing that I was watching! I had brought with me from the UK a cross stitch kit, a very large kit with two clowns. I decided this was the time to start it. So, most days after breakfast and any shopping and household chores, the boys would skip off to the park and I would drag a chair outside and grab my cross stitching. We lived on the first floor at that time above a housewares shop that was run by my landlord. I could see 90% of the park so I was happy to let them enjoy.

After a few weeks, I started to see the boys interacting more and more with the Turkish kids that were playing in the park. When the boys came in on an evening I would ask them about the kids and the interactions, and was amazed that my boys knew so much! I would ask how they knew and it became evident that my kids were speaking Turkish. How? How could they know Turkish? Over the following weeks, months even, I would ask the boys how they knew what the Turkish kids were saying 'We just do' was always their reply. How do you know what to say I would ask, 'We just do' was always their reply! Even now, I am amazed and astounded that they learned the language so well and so quickly. At the end of the school holidays, they were both able to start attending the local council school and from that day forward, never had any issues with their language. Today, they still speak Turkish when they are both home at the same time. They don't do it when they are downstairs, but if they are upstairs and on their games, for example, they can be heard chattering away in Turkish. They always argue in Turkish!

In Turkey, they would always speak English in whichever apartment we lived in, but there was a switch in their heads and as they stepped through the doorway into the corridor to leave home, they would instantly start speaking Turkish. They never even realised they were doing it. If we were out, and an English person spoke to them in Turkish, they genuinely couldn't answer in Turkish, and if a Turk spoke to them in English they couldn't answer in English. It was a weird, unfathomable thing, which just can't be explained.

The boys looked like Turks, strange thing to say I know, but they had the looks. Since we lived there, they went black from being outside so much. Even if I lathered them in sun cream their tans were amazing. As they grew, instead of wearing the English clothes I'd brought with us, they were wearing clothes that were bought in Turkey, so they 'fitted in'.

We had so much fun when we were in cafes. The waiters would approach us, they would look from the boys to me and then back to the boys. I had a great tan all the time I lived in Turkey but my clothing and style was, I guess, still European. Now, if the waiters asked us for our order in Turkish, I would answer in English but the boys would speak Turkish to each other! If they asked for our order in Turkish I would answer in Turkish and the boys would speak English! I know, I know, simple things for simple minds but it made me and the kids laugh so much. We would eventually 'let on' to the waiters who would stand and talk to us, sometimes before we let on, they would tell me my English was really good, where did I study? People in general loved to talk to us all, asking so many questions about where we came from, what we were doing in Turkey and loads more. Even then the boys were 'buggers'. When asked their names, they would always, ALWAYS give some random name, any name but their own!

Alanya Blood Drive

I was living in Turkey when they had a major earthquake in 1999. Whether it was just a coincidence or related, I'll never know, but all the electricity in Alanya went off for at least 12 hours. At that time, the city had a loud speaker system and various things were announced over it, such as names of people being buried, concerts, and other such news items. This particular day, the day after the earthquake, the announcements were appealing for blood donors, and for people to contribute shoes as many victims of the earthquake had run into the streets in bare feet.

The boys and I managed to come up with a couple of pairs of unused training shoes, and I decided to donate blood. I knew I had 'O' Negative blood which is called the 'universal donor' and everyone can use it, so off I went, blood in arm, to the local government hospital.

Nervous isn't the word for this, but I got off the bus and walked into the hospital, without a clue about what would happen or where. However, I was shown into a small room and almost instantly sat down. The blood was leaving my arm within minutes of arriving at the hospital. I'd done my little bit, and after that day I would regularly ride up to the hospital and give blood.

On one of the following trips, I was a little freaked out, however. This time I could speak a little more Turkish and was having a chat with the nurse taking my blood. The room was really sad, the blood banks were just a small cupboard, and were almost always empty. Today was no exception, and I asked the nurse how they coped. What happened when they had no blood? She explained that normally families would come into hospital with anyone involved in an accident, or when they might need blood during an operation. Everyone in the family would give blood. If there wasn't enough of the right type donated, they would ask the staff in the hospital, the porters, nurses, security staff and even visitors, to donate!

She explained that there was, at the same time that we were chatting, a young man in theatre undergoing an operation. He needed lots of blood transfusions, and that's where my blood would be going. I sat quietly until they had taken their bag-full, and then, as they were taking the needle out of my arm, a middle-aged man appeared at the door. He snatched the bag of blood out of the nurse's hand and he ran away down the corridor.

I was given a drink and the nurse asked me to wait a few minutes before I left. I asked who the man was and she explained that she had called the theatre to tell them she was getting more blood for them. The theatre had sent the man to collect the blood. It must have gone into the young man in theatre while it was still warm. No time for tests of any kind.

I went home and was a little in shock as to how that could happen, but if I helped in any small way to save a life, I was pleased.

I continued to give blood for a few years, but never again did I see it running down to theatre.

Sunnet Party

The boys might not thank me for offering the following information, but I'd like to share this as it was a fabulous day. When we were still living in the UK, both boys had problems with their foreskins and my then GP, a lovely man, knew that the boys were being brought up as Muslims. He also knew that we did at some point intend to move to Turkey. He advised me that if I wanted him to recommend circumcision for them both as a local hospital, he would be happy to, but that the operation would probably be undertaken by a trainee or newly qualified doctor. He told me that, if he were me, he would wait until we moved to Turkey and have the operation done there. It was done millions of times, by doctors who knew exactly how to compete the operation quickly and competently.

We followed his advice and after we had been in Turkey for a year we decided that now was the time, before Aslan was too old. Through my circle of friends we were put in contact with 'the man'. Not a doctor, but he was registered to carry out circumcisions. We did change things slightly as Turks carried these out at restaurants or party venues. I just couldn't do that, so we arranged to have the party and then for 'the man' to visit the boys at our home.

A friend, who managed a fabulous hotel in Alanya called the Grand Kaptan, let us arrange the party there. It was mid-season and there would be tourist there, but that was all the more fun. An American friend called Charlotte was a singer, and she would be performing that same night. That was great, as Charlotte knew the boys.

I bought Sunnet outfits, navy blue trousers, new smart black shoes, white shirts with frills down the front, navy blue waistcoats, blue dickie bows, a navy cape with white fur trimming, a wonderful hat with the same fur trimming, a sceptre, again in the same colours and theme. A blue cummerbund and a sash with Mashallah on it. The whole point of the Sunnet party, or the day preceding it, was that the young boy would be prince for the day.

We hired a jeep and trimmed it up with balloons. A friend offered to drive us, and we left home a couple of hours before the party was due. Erkan and I sat in the jeep with them, and we drove around Alanya.It was summer, almost the end of the school holidays, and there were tourist around. There were people following us in their own cars and as we drove around, the boys reluctantly stood up and everyone pipped their car horns and cheered out of the car windows. The tourists even joined in clapping and shouting, even though I'm sure they had no idea what was happening!

We called at the photographer's and another friend's boyfriend took some amazing photos of both boys, photos I still have today. We opted for something a little different as most Sunnet pictures are just one large photo on canvas, we decided to have several photos framed and mounted in two different frames.

We arrived at the hotel where we had invited about 30 people, so we headed to the garden where tourist were already seated and we took our places. Part of the Sunnet party was that the boys would be presented with gold and money by friends and family, they did actually like that idea! The usual form of gold that was given would be a little charm, sometimes a small coin, sometimes an animal or a figure. These were pinned onto the lapel of their waistcoats, as their cloaks were flung off at the first opportunity! Even the tourists in the hotel were coming forward and having photos taken with the boys, then giving them cash and wishing them all the best.

We had a lovely party, Charlotte was belting her songs out, we had fireworks and a fabulous cake, shared by everyone. Before the party was finished we made our apologies, said bye to everyone and headed home. The deed had yet to be done. 'The man' turned up a few minutes before we left the hotel and he quickly grabbed some food and a drink and advised us how he wanted to proceed. We discovered later that evening that he had already attended 6 Sunnet parties that day!

Once we arrived home the boys were split up, Kaan staying in a bedroom with me, and Aslan going with his Dad, I was so frightened but was trying to stay calm for Kaan's sake. Surprisingly quickly, Aslan appeared in the doorway of the bedroom, grinning and saying 'didn't hurt at all Kaan'. Kaan then zipped off with his Dad, leaving Aslan with me. Aslan had a pair of cotton boxer shorts on, and he was holding the front of the shorts out so they didn't touch him. He spent the next three days wandering around the apartment doing that! When Kaan reappeared, he was exactly the same, they both took the deed in their stride! They had been given a local anaesthetic, and even when it wore off they were little troopers, and hardly complained over the next few days. They healed quickly, no problems, and we have a fantastic day to remember. My GP back in the UK was spot on with his advice! The thing that truly stays in my mind however was 'the man', who, while clearing up his equipment, held up two 'things' in his hand. Naively, I didn't really have a clue what he had. Then what he said was translated, and he had been saying I could make a lovely pair of earrings! It might seem a little barbaric to some of you reading this, but truly, it was done in a clean, safe way, the boys were 'Princes' for the day, which was part of their culture, and they were really OK with it all.

A Passion For Turkey

I was lucky enough to meet several ex-pat British girls when I moved to Turkey. I'm not sure how I met the first one, but we all got together fairly quickly. We had to stick together and it was good to have friends.

I'm ashamed to say that during the course of my ten years in Turkey, I gained many friends but then sometimes lost track of them, depending where in my chaotic, crazy life I was. I hid from some of them, I avoided some of them during the worst times. I lost a good friend due to a marriage. But I would like to say a word to every friend I made in Turkey, some are still living out there, some back in their home countries now. Well ladies, it was a privilege to know you all.

We attended meetings. I think it was every week, but I might be lying about the frequency, but we all got together regularly. It was great. Some had children a similar age to mine, and some had babies, so it was a good way to share help and information, especially to the newly arriving girls.

It was a good time, and this group had been originally formed by Lynda and Avril. But over the years as with most things, other people started attending and then taking over. Some though that kids shouldn't have been allowed, some just had their heads up their arses. There were a lot of married couples with a good income that had retired out there. They needed something different from the group we had, but instead of starting their own group, our friendly, useful and wonderful little group was swallowed up. The girls with kids just stopped going, I stopped going before I said something that I might have regretted.

However, back when the group was friendly and helpful, we decided that we needed a small handout or booklet that we could give to the newbies when they arrived, to help them along. I'd already written a couple of items for a basic newsletter that we had, so I accepted the request to write it. Those were the days before everyone had a PC, laptop or some other kind of electronic device. Some girls had desk top computers, but not many. So, I found an Internet café close to home, and after the boys had gone to school, I started my information booklet. I'd been in Turkey for a while when this was happening, and I'd done quite a lot by then. We'd moved into an apartment, I tried to decorate, I shopped, paid bills, dealt with travelling, and lots of other things you would normally take for granted.

I sat typing day after day, and I quickly realised that I knew more than I thought. Putting everything I knew already into a little handout was impossible. I made the decision to write a proper book. Ha, just like that! So, I did. I also organised the basic information into a good handout size, and got that ready for the group to produce and give out. Then I went to town on my book. I had plans. I needed plans as I didn't have any cash to print books, but first I approached the local bank, my bank, and the hospital who I knew from experience were very good with foreigners. I explained to both of them what I was doing, and surprisingly, I was able to obtain sponsorship from both businesses to have advertisements on the inside and outside covers, of my as yet uncompleted book. I approached a gold shop I knew, a leather shop I knew, and a restaurant. Between these businesses I managed to scrape up enough money to have 1000 of these little paperback books printed. I sat with the guys in the printers for two or three days and we went through the book putting in images and cartoons. And it was printed off with a red cover and was proudly called a 'Passion for Turkey' the first printing, much to my surprise, cost me nothing. It was all covered by sponsorship. Way to go Tina!

I started selling them, to the ex-pats and to tourists. I later sold them to my Diamond Irish friend. She had started selling properties in Alanya to other people in Ireland, on behalf of the guy she'd bought her apartment from. She took loads of books from me, and she gave them out on her sales stand to potential customers. The builder would fly her a stand out, and she would attend the big property fayres when the Irish had lots of spare cash, before the financial crash in 2007.

When I had a computer and the Internet, I would advertise them on a website which was specifically designed for girls who had Turkish boyfriends or husbands. I started a blog and added a lot of stories and articles as well as funny pictures. Eventually, I had a large following and could sell books via there too. I did well with that naïve little book. It was reprinted many times.

Nothing to do with my little book, but I was once interviewed by a newly established magazine that was being produced in Alanya, called 'Hello Alanya'. It was produced in English on one page and in Dutch on the other. They interviewed Ex-pats in every issue, and I think I was in the second issue. During that interview they discovered I had written my little book, so then I was asked if I would write an article for them each month. They couldn't pay very much, but every little helped back then. I agreed, and wrote several articles for them. I appeared regularly in 'Hello Alanya', for maybe a year. The funniest thing was that there was a small photo of me in the front of the magazine, as there were with all the contributors and editors etc. I started being recognised! Oh my goodness, fame at last!

This then lead to being approached by an English property magazine and I wrote them an article about buying and renting property.

I'd forgotten about all this until I started digging into my memories to write this book. I still have copies of those magazines somewhere. I might go find them and check them out again!

Whilst I've been writing this book, and whilst David has been diligently editing it and putting in commas and full stops for me, I stopped for a moment and said, 'Who on earth will believe all this happened. I am struggling, and I was in it'!

Mum and Dad Down The Road

We, as a family, moved out to Turkey in November 1998. It was a tough decision to make at any time, but it was what we thought would give us a better standard of life with the boys. It was very sad to leave Mum and Dad.

I have an older brother who I haven't spoken to since my youngest son was a couple of months old. He and my Mum and Dad had a fall out one Christmas, and I got caught in the middle of it. I tried to build a bridge before we moved out to Turkey but my brother simply didn't want to know, so I left for Turkey with no brother as far as I was concerned. You'll see later on why I don't care if I never see him again!

We stayed in contact with Mum and Dad as best as we were able to, although this was before facetime, skype and all the internet tools we have now. The following May, Mum and Dad came out to visit us, we were still living in the hotel then, and Mum and Dad stayed in one of the rooms near ours. We had managed to find a few 'random' guests and the pool was open, as was the bar and restaurant, but it was very sparse and certainly was not making anyone a living!

During that time Mum very quickly picked up on the fact that Erkan and I were not the close loving couple we had been when we left the UK. She didn't know then that it had become abusive, although she did threaten to hurt Erkan if she found out he had ever hurt me of the boys!

Shortly after Mum and Dad's first visit, Erkan, the boys and I moved into a small apartment in Alanya. It was an old apartment, but it was our starting place.

Mum and Dad visited four times during 1999, and were out in Turkey for the 2000 New Year. They both loved Alanya, they clearly missed the boys and in return the boys missed them. They had looked after the boys in the UK when I had returned to work, and were a major part of each other's lives!

My Dad was a character. He loved to sit on the balcony and watch the world go by. On Fridays the road beneath my apartment was the market; activity would start very early in the morning and end late at night. Dad loved it! There was one particular pick-up truck which used to turn up so loaded with fruit and veg, it was to the point where Dad was convinced that the wheels would buckle and give way. There was a cola bottle fastened to the roof, and that was full of fuel, with a pipe down to the fuel tank! We never did find out what that was all about.

The same stall holder was also on Dad's watch-list when he came to visit, as they had a blonde son. Not unheard of in Turkey, but very rare and Dad was convinced it was Ben Needham, a little English boy who had been lost/kidnapped from a Greek Island when on holiday. Dad thought we should contact some police force somewhere, but he never did.

We had the boys Sunnet whilst Mum and Dad were out there holidaying. We tried to be as 'normal' as possible but sometimes Erkan would be absent for a couple of days at a time, and I always excused his absence by saying something had occurred in the hotel which he had to deal with. In truth Erkan had very little dealing with the hotel, our 'business' partner was dealing with it all with his son, and we had been cut out of it. Erkan was bringing a small amount of money home, and I was undertaking a couple of airport transfers a week so we were managing, but only just…

During the New Year's holiday, Mum and Dad told me that they had decided to move out to Alanya. I was shocked, incredibly shocked. I had been born in the house they still lived in. I never thought they would move from there to anywhere. But they went on to explain that my brother was still not talking to them, although he only lived about 8 houses further along the road from the house Mum and Dad's house. He had banned his kids, Mum and Dad's grandkids, from visiting them, so what reason did they have to they stay there?

To this day I still think they also knew I was struggling in many ways, but also knew I wasn't ready to give it in and move back to the UK, so that was probably a large part of their move.

They stuck to their word! They went home to the UK, put in the visa applications to allow them to live in Turkey with no problems and put the house up for sale. It sold incredibly quickly. It was a lovely house, they lived in Yorkshire, in a small village next to the miner's village where Dad had worked. It was an ex council house, situated on a corner with a large well maintained garden; lilac trees, rose bushes, lawns and a hawthorn hedge all the way round so it had lots of privacy. They had changed windows, extended it and kept it in extremely good order. It was sold within 6 weeks, but sadly this was just before the housing boom. But they still said they were happy with the price they got, and that it sold quickly avoiding long and complicated waits.

They came back to Turkey in February and found an apartment to live in. They decided to rent which I always thought was the best decision, and their apartment was about 5 minutes walk away from the Cleopatra beach, which is one of the best beaches in Turkey. It was a 10 – 15 minute walk from my own apartment and was owned by a nice landlord.

They moved out lock stock and barrel before 1st April! They had a good life in Turkey, they had arranged for my Dad's miner's pension to continue to be paid to them, but through their Turkish bank account. They were both in good health, and they were able to live like Kings! Dad got a bicycle, he really wanted a little moped, but Mum was really against that as the traffic in Alanya at that time was bonkers at best, and totally lunatic at worst.

Mum and Dad helped me with the boys for many reasons. After my divorce from Erkan, I hit a period of time that I can only call a melt-down. If it hadn't been a good friend of mine called Jules, I don't know what I would have done. I had hit rock bottom, I was angry with everyone. Jules had problems of her own, which is why she moved out to Turkey with her youngest son. We spent the whole of one season going out and getting drunk! I always feel that Mum and Dad trusted me, and they instinctively knew that I needed to get through this horrible period in my life. They never complained about how I was conducting myself, and they were happy to look after the boys for me. When the season ended I just snapped out of whatever it was, the black dog of depression had started following someone else about and I was 'back to normal', whatever normal was.

During that crazy season Jules and I got into a few scrapes, met a lot of odd people, and healed each other. I will always be grateful to that lady. I have put a chapter together about some of our outrageous evenings out. Some are totally unbelievable, but trust me, we were out of control!

Mum and Dad were happy when I met Cevat, he was good with them, he sent his drivers to take them shopping on the market, he helped them sort any problems they had with anything or anybody. We even had a few days holiday away with him. They were great, and learned to adapt and live easily within the community, there were no other foreigners living in their apartment block, but the Turks took them under their wings. They never did learn more than a couple of words of Turkish though!

The boys, at the weekends and during the school holidays, would head to the harbour where they could fish. They had a little money to buy bait, they had a lunch packed up, and I knew they wouldn't be back for several hours. Once they were older, it was a great place to grow up. I never worried about them being attacked by other kids, or being abducted by a weirdo. I knew where they were and they were as safe as they could be. I'd been down to the harbour a few times randomly to check on them and they were in the middle of the group of Turkish men who were fishing and were fine. To confirm this, my Dad regularly used to make the boys extra food, pack it up and cycle down to the harbour to feed them and spend some time. The first few times he did this, the Turkish fishermen got a little anxious about an 'old English man' trying to chat with two 'Turkish boys'. Once the boys had explained a few times that he wasn't weird, that he was actually their Grandfather, the Turks took to him and my Dad became 'one of them'!

In February 2005 Mum, Dad and myself attended a hospital appointment. Dad had been feeling ill a short while and had attended a few appointments at the local private hospital. I know the date because it was my birthday. Such a sad day. Dad was diagnosed with cancer. Terminal cancer! Such a big strong man, and he was still trying to be strong to keep my Mum from smashing into a million pieces. I'm not going into his illness, just to say that after a dose of Chemo, we were sitting in a nice café high on the hills behind Alanya, when he told Mum and I that he didn't want any more Chemo as it was probably worse than the illness. He wanted to die on his own terms.

As he became ill to the point that he was in bed, Mum was trying to nurse him herself. There were no MacMillan nurses there, no home care, no one, and Dad didn't want to be in a hospital where he couldn't understand or speak to anyone. We found a lady, another ex-pat who had worked in care homes and hospices, and she started to help Mum. She knew what was coming next, and with her help we were able to keep Dad at home.

This is where I 'divorced' my brother for good. He hadn't made any attempt to contact Mum or Dad during the 5 years they had lived in Turkey. One of my Uncles, Mum's brother, had visited Mum and Dad, so my brother was quite able to track them down but he never bothered. When Dad was towards the end of his life, I decided, and it was no small thing, to contact my brother. It was on my conscience. If I contacted him and he said who cares, my conscience was clear, if I didn't contact him then I would have felt bad for the rest of my life. I phoned my Uncle in the UK, without telling my Mum. My Uncle visited my brother and told him how ill Dad was. The result? Well, a couple of swear words! When I was told, I don't think I was surprised. I didn't tell Mum, she was upset enough. I do wish now though, that I had lied to my Dad when he was bed ridden and told him that his only son had called to say he loved him and ask about him.

Dad died that August. I'd had to organise many things weeks before he died, which still haunt me when I think back.

Muslims, don't use coffins, they are swaddled instead, and they are also buried within 24 hours. Even before Dad died I had to find the Turks' equivalent of an undertaker. Everything was so complicated. We had to gain authority for Dad to be buried in the 'Foreigners' graveyard. I had to arrange for a coffin to be built specially, and there was no way of having a service as there were no churches in Alanya. The best hope we had at the time of my Dad's passing would be to ask all my friends with hotels or restaurants, as well as my rep friends, if they knew of a Vicar, a priest or anyone who would say some words over Dad's grave when the time came!

I was working the day Dad passed. I was several miles away and Mum called to say come home. I was a few minutes late and bitterly regret that too, but I had to work and Mum understood. The 'undertaker' arranged for Dad to be collected, and his body was taken to the Morgue near the graveyard. The 'funeral' was to take place the following day so my life was then thrown into overdrive. Those friends who had said they would help when the time came all did their part. A German priest was found, who, even though he was on his holiday, agreed to attend and say a few words for Dad. I visited many florists until I found one who could make what I needed, which was a cushion type arrangement for Mum to leave, and a huge bunch of lilies for the boys and I to leave for Dad. I do remember having an argument with one florist, it was over Christians and Muslims, I can't really remember the context, but I do remember that I was in the street screaming before I gave in and got into my car and moved on. Friends were notified of the times, and I had asked some Irish friends of mine with a pub if they would be able to put something together food-wise on short notice, for people when they left the graveyard.

That day went as good as it might. Bearing in mind that the Priest had never met Dad, I thought that I needed to say some words over his grave, which were the hardest words I've ever put on paper and said. Even though I was speaking to friends, good friends, it wasn't at all easy. I told them that the old English man was the man who everyone knew. The one who was always whistling, the happy man, the man willing to share

61

anything he had, the husband, the father and the best Grandad ever.

The priest spoke, I spoke, we cried, we laid flowers on top of the grave, then we went to the pub and had a drink and saw Dad off on his way!

The following day, one of my nephews called Mum. I don't know how they got the number, from my Uncle I'm guessing. Mum explained that they were a few days late. They, there were two of the three grandsons speaking, wanted to go out to see Nana. Great she said until it unfolded that they also wanted to bring girlfriends with them, stay with Mum and have a holiday. Mum respectfully said she couldn't put them up as her apartment was too small. But she could recommend a hotel. The boys were never heard of again. But a couple of days later, Mum received a weird letter from my sister-in-law. Not once did the letter mention Dad or his illness, or ask Mum if she was OK. It went something like 'Me, me me, we, them, me, me me and me'. Mum had never had a great relationship with her daughter-in-law, the reason for arguing with her son had been something to do with his wife wanting something they couldn't afford in the first place. Mum showed me the letter when I was there and asked what I thought. Well, I thought it was a selfish, uncaring piece of shit letter. Mum laughed and said she agreed. It was put in the bin.

Over the years, even though we since came back to the UK, Mum and I really don't wish to speak to my brother, he'd had chances to build bridges. His sons, who by then were young men, not kids, had their chance too. On Facebook one of them put out a post saying he was looking for his Nan, who used to live in Turkey. A friend warned me, and I blocked the whole family after speaking with Mum. She didn't want to see any of them. He hadn't even got Mum and Dad's forenames right!

My boys were sent messages through Facebook too. They spoke to Mum and I before blocking them. Their response was 'where were they when Nan needed them?'

Some people might say, we did wrong, we should make peace, we should forgive. But when asked now, Mum only has a daughter and I don't have a brother. I'm bitter about having a twat for a brother, who let his Dad die without even lifting the phone and dialling a few numbers.

Mum stayed in Turkey, she eventually moved in with me and later moved back to the UK with me. She lives a few miles away in a small bungalow, but a long way from Yorkshire now.

When I visit Alanya, I always go 'see' my Dad, his place of rest is really nice now. We had a marble grave surround made for him, with a headstone. He's in a lovely place, with bougainvillea bushes and olive trees shading his grave. The graveyard is full now, and it is being maintained to a very high standard. White gravel has been put down between the graves, and the whole site is planted up and kept in great order. A friend of mine, the English lady, Avril, who had started the ex-pat group, is a few metres away. She caused a frenzy, and would have loved it. She died whilst visiting friends and family in the UK. She was cremated in the UK with a service for her family, and her Turkish boyfriend brought her ashes back to Turkey to be buried. The Turkish press got hold of the story, and the graveyard was overrun with them trying to get a picture of the ashes being buried. Cremations don't happen in Turkey and the whole occasion was very odd for Turks.

I often think of the write-up Dad got in the papers after his death, he would have found it very funny. He was a coal miner for all of his life. The Turkish Newspapers had him working for the British Consulate. He would have laughed!

I also regret that Mum will never get back to Turkey. She's not well enough to travel on a plane and really hasn't been for many years. The boys can't go back until they get their passports sorted. They both have dual nationality and they are both still required to do National Service in the Turkish army. This means that they can't go back to Turkey without being arrested, even though they are both serving in the British Army, which is ironic. It is possible to buy your way out of National Service if you are resident in another country. We have spoken about sorting it out a few times, and I hope we can. One day I'd love a family holiday with them, and I'd love them to go see Dad. I do sit and tell him all about them though. He would be so proud!

The Crafters

As part of my wide and varied job choices and options when I lived in Turkey, I was really up for trying anything that I could make money at, and could obviously do competently. But this one was very odd.

I'd wandered around Alanya enough to know that on Saturdays and Sundays every week, throughout the entire year, a group of Turkish ladies could be found with tables covered by varied and brightly coloured umbrellas. They were in the car park of the huge council building that overlooked the harbour in Alanya. I had wandered around often because I love crafts and homemade goods. The boys used to fish from some huge boulders that had been put into the harbour to form sea walls, so I would often sit and watch the world go by as they fished.

I was desperate for a means of making money, but I could knit and I could cross stitch. One day I had the absurd notion that maybe I could make something that I could sell on a weekend with these ladies. At home, I had a knitting pattern for scarecrow dolls. I hadn't seen any of the ladies selling anything like dolls or knitted toys, so I bought some wool and had a go. I knew that it's impossible to ever get back a fair price for hand made goods, as labour is rarely taken into account, but what if I could make these dolls during the week and on a night when I was on my own, then sell them on weekends? If I made a profit of any kind then I was winning.

I made my first scarecrow, I bought a cheap bed pillow, and used the stuffing to fill it. It hadn't taken as long as I thought it might, there were lots of tiny pieces but nothing complicated. I was happy with it, it was bright and unusual. The following weekend I approached a couple of women at the craft market. My Turkish was still dodgy and limited, and once again I was learning words and phrases for something different. We struggled through, and a couple of the ladies were particularly helpful. I think they thought I was being a little foolish at first, in their eyes why on earth would an English woman want to do what they did? Eventually they explained that as a 'newbie' I would be required to turn up early on a morning. I needed a table, an umbrella and a chair. If there was a free place for me to set up, I could. There was no rent to pay, but it was monitored by the council, and only hand made goods were allowed to be displayed and sold. I think they were shocked at the thought that an English woman could 'make' anything.

The following week, with about 9 completed scarecrows in a huge bag. I had a fold-up table out of my kitchen, and two boys carrying fishing gear. We boarded the council bus and headed to town. It wasn't easy, but Aslan was growing up and he helped me whilst Kaan had the fishing stuff. We arrived early and stood patiently, the women seemed to be collecting their tables, chairs and umbrellas from somewhere local and in no time at all they were laying out their goods; Jewellery, knitted clothing, children's wear. Crocheting - lots and lots of crocheting, towel edging, doilies, table cloths, all items I am still in awe of. They beckoned me over and I was allowed to set up. It was a very hot day and I had no umbrella, but the ladies on either side of me, slightly moved theirs so I wasn't in the full sunshine. I laid out my dolls and they were quite a hit with the ladies. More importantly, by the end of the weekend I had sold them all. Overnight I had been able to store my table in a room in a nearby underground car park with the other ladies' things, which was a massive help, but it was still hard work.

To cut a long story short, it took me a long time to convince the ladies that I would turn up every weekend, but eventually I was given a permanent spot. I could then leave my table, a chair and an umbrella there, so all I needed to carry was the dolls. I was knitting, sewing and stuffing dolls every minute of the day when I wasn't earning money doing something else. I was able to produce 14 / 15 a week on my own, but boy it was tiring. I attended that market for about two years. When Mum moved to Turkey she started helping me and used to 'knit' the scarecrow's straw hair, which was very fiddly and time-consuming. When I opened my little shop, I sat in the shop during the weekdays, and I knitted. The scarecrows went on the shelves of my shop, and the ones which weren't sold went to the fayre at the weekend. I had developed my scarecrow pattern, and I could make footballers of varying colours. I made brides, grooms and an upside down doll which when tipped upside down would be a blond hair doll and the other way would be a dark haired doll. I even paid 3 or 4 Turkish ladies to knit parts for me. With Mum's help I increased the numbers I was selling, and I was making more money. Hard work though. I was woken more than once by the boys getting up for school because I had been sitting knitting in my chair in front of the TV, fallen asleep, and never managed to get to bed.

I also made baby clothes from English patterns I had. They were popular because the style was completely different to the Turkish style. I tried a few cross stitch items, but they were slower to sell. I tried some glass painting which was good as it was far quicker to make. That sold, but it proved difficult to move it to the fayre very easily on the bus!

During my time on that fayre I made amazing friendships with those ladies, even with one particular lady who thought I was just messing about and told everyone that I wouldn't stick it out. She became a very good friend. They got to know the boys, as the boys would help me set up and then stay nearby on the harbour, fishing. They came back occasionally for food, or money for a drink. The ladies always gave them something, even though I had packed food up for us. The boys were given cakes and biscuits. The ladies were so gracious, as none of us had very much. Some were widows, some had husbands with illness or disabilities, some of us were just broke and trying to make ends meet.

During my time on there, a friend's husband, Sirdir, was a rep with Saga. He was a lovely, quietly spoken man, and he turned up one Saturday morning and told me he had added my stall onto his excursion around Alanya! I thought it was very funny, I never sold anything to any of his guests, and I tried to explain to him that most of the women with him were probably making their own scarecrows at home. I did answer a million questions though as to why I was there. Husband? Kids? The questions were endless. I was happy for them to visit though, as the other ladies benefitted from the visitors.

We were there through all weather, good and bad, hot and cold, and when I eventually found work that I could do full time and make enough money to stop knitting, I was actually rather sad.

I continued to visit them every chance I got, and if I had cash I would always buy something, amethyst pendants being a favourite. Even now I'm back in the UK, I always visit them at least once if I'm on holiday in Alanya. I buy several items and try and buy from different women to share it out. But I have discovered it's harder for them now. The council now provides special little stalls which have drawers and storage underneath so the ladies don't have to carry their stock daily, they have put lighting up and a cover so the ladies are out of the weather. But now they pay rent, they have to work until 10pm at least, and they told me that sometimes they are there much later to get everything put away. They now have to ask for permission from the council to miss a day, and they are there every day, not just the weekends. So they are sitting at their stalls trying to make a sale, whilst at the same time trying to make new stock! Harsh, very harsh!

If one day I have a big lottery win, I would visit that craft fayre and the ladies who are still there. The ones who had helped me and the boys way back would never need to work another day in their lives.

If you ever visit Alanya, please walk down to the harbour front, across the road from the Council Tea Gardens and up near the council buildings, and you will see a stretch of covered stalls, all manned by nice people trying to make a living. Be kind, be generous and make their day! And yours!

The Fight Club

This is a difficult part for me to write but it's a big part of me, it's probably got a lot to do with how I am and who I am now. It's amazing in the fact that I got through it, that I got through it without going mad, without committing suicide, without it turning me into a blithering wreck for longer than it did. I got through it.

Once Erkan and I had moved to Turkey, things quickly, and I mean quickly, changed. In the UK we had a partnership. Once back in Turkey he moved into the Captain's position. Never before had he questioned where I was going. At first, I assumed it was because we were in Turkey, in a new, strange place, but there was more to it than that. He would ask why I was putting makeup on. In the UK I never stepped out of the house without full makeup on, but when in Turkey, even in the Winter months, it was too hot to bother. The makeup would just run off. I stopped using most of the makeup I had, but continued to use a little eye liner and lipstick. This would be questioned, and I used to laugh as I answered.

Some of my clothing choices were questioned too. I was always respectful when we took holidays in Turkey, and I had never been a woman to wear low cut or revealing clothes anyway. Slowly this inquisition was becoming an everyday part of our lives, and it was becoming very bloody annoying. I had given him the benefit of the doubt at first. Now I didn't know what his motive to ask was. One evening I was about to leave the apartment, I can't recall the reason, but that wasn't important. As I was leaving I got the usual list of questions; where was I going, why was I dressed like that, and the corker.. why was I made up like a tart? Never had he spoken to me like that before. Where the hell had my loving, helpful, thoughtful husband gone? I think I'd reached the point where I would no longer make excuses in my head for him to be like this. I wanted to know why. I spun around, he wasn't standing very far from me and I asked 'What the Hell Erkan, what are all the bloody questions about?' Before I knew it, Erkan had slapped me across the face, and his reply was something like 'Answer the questions or stay in.' I was stunned, both at the slap and at the comment.

I was so glad that the boys were outside playing. I walked into the bedroom and quietly closed the door. I was in a daze and I wanted to cry, I so wanted to cry. My face was stinging, and I was hurting in more ways than I can ever describe. I so wanted Erkan to walk into the bedroom and be full of remorse, to apologise and ask me to forgive him, but it didn't happen then, and it never happened at all throughout the rest of our time together.

The boys came in shortly afterwards and I tried my best to remain calm, not to show the mark on my cheek that I'd ended up with, and to just get through the evening. We had dinner, then Erkan left without a word to any of us.

Now I had read about, watched programmes on TV, and generally heard about abused women. Of course, I felt sorry for anyone living in such circumstances, wondering why they didn't leave, why do they put up with it? Were they stupid? The answer in my case was learned the hard way.

I'm not going into every detail, as this book is to entertain, not to depress or make you feel sorry for me. But that first slap opened some kind of portal that led into about 18 months of hell. It led me into not answering my phone when friends rang. It led me to not answering my door, or at least to hardly anyone. It led me to start using makeup again, but this time to cover up marks and bruises.

I tried, I tried so hard, to stop this happening in front of the boys. For the first few months I became docile and non-argumentative, but there would always be something. Erkan was going out during the day. He brought money home some days, but other days there was nothing and those were the worst days. Slaps turned into punching, and bruises were appearing on my forearms and other parts of my body. He had seemed to learn that leaving visible marks on my face wasn't a clever idea, as it meant I wouldn't be able to work on my airport transfers.

The boys, I'm sure, knew what was happening but didn't understand. They grew closer to me, and I'm sure that it was their protective side coming to the surface. They were only little boys, but I'm sure that's what it was.

I was slowly cutting myself off from everyone. I didn't want to explain the bruising, I didn't want to break into floods of tears in the middle of a 'normal' conversation. I had turned into a blithering wreck. I had turned into one of these women I had seen, read and heard about. But how the hell had that happened?

I didn't know this for a long time, but it turned out that each day Erkan wasn't actually going off to the job I thought he had. By then we had rented two small shops, one for me as a craft shop, and one for him which we had equipped as a repair shop with basic tools. However, when I walked around to my little shop after the boys had left for school, he was never in his. I thought that at least he was working and bringing a small amount home most evenings. But he was actually gambling. I discovered that when it was all too late.

It turned out that he would walk around to one of the gambling cafes, the ones where groups of men can be see playing backgammon. But inside these cafes they are playing poker and gambling for serious money.

During all of this time, apart from backing away from my friends and lying so much, everyday life continued as best it could. I had my little shop and my knitting. The boys went to school and came home, and if we were on our own we would have a good time. If Erkan was home, we would all naturally stay quieter and out of his way.

I was getting slapped a lot, the more it happened, the more I retreated a little further into myself. I stopped trying to argue back, I stopped thinking about the future anymore, the future looked very bleak. All I thought about was the here and now, getting through each day, and trying to make life for the boys as normal as I could. I have to say though, that Erkan never once hurt the boys physically.

What he did do was something almost as bad, though. On one particularly bad day, the boys had gone fishing and I had closed my shop for the day and was home. Erkan suddenly appeared, in a bit of a state about something. He used the bathroom then came to me in the kitchen. He wanted money, and I gave him my purse, but I had already learned not to keep much money in there as it vanished on a daily basis. I started hiding any money I had, either in the shop or in the kitchen cupboards.

Erkan tipped my purse out and swore when he saw how little was in there. He walked off. I heard him in other rooms and then I heard the door bang as he left the apartment. In a sudden flash, and even now I don't know where the flash came from, I had a thought and ran into the bedroom to check my jewellery box. It should have contained, along with my junk jewellery, a couple of gold necklaces, one with a small gold ingot on it. There should have been a very heavy bracelet, again with a little gold trinket fastened onto it, a pair of gold hoop earrings, and my engagement ring. My engagement ring wasn't a normal ring, it had been made for me many years ago during a trip to Izmir. It was 18ct gold and was a hand that wrapped round my finger and in the palm of that hand there was a tiny ruby. Describing it here, it sounds awful, but it was a really nicely designed and made ring. Anyway, none of the gold was where it should be!

Then another panic gripped me, in one of the drawers in the bedroom, was an envelope. It should have contained the boy's gold. During their Sunnet party, friends and family approached the boys and pinned gold onto the lapels of their waistcoats. These presents would have been stored away until they needed something and I could have sold them to pay for whatever they needed. Some were little coins, some were figures, some were lucky Turkish eyes surrounded by gold. But all were gold, and all were gone.

This somehow clicked a switch in my head. He had taken from his own children, what was he doing? He never reappeared for the rest of that day. The boys came home and for the three of us it was business as normal, they told me about their day, their catches and their near misses. I loved those boys so much.

The day after that, the kids had gone to school and I was getting ready to head to my shop and was making a sandwich to take with me when Erkan appeared. He looked scruffy, he needed a shave badly, his long hair was lank and greasy and I think he'd been wearing his clothes for several days.

That was it, I lost it and I lost it big time. Everything I'd been bottling up, everything I'd been trying to hide, everything I really thought about the way he had treated me and his children came out. I remember screaming at him, I was truly at the end of my tether. The beating I got in return was spectacular, it was like a badly made film. The consequences of that day, caused me to go into a traumatic menopause. I was barely 40. No more periods, but no hot flushes or other symptoms. Sometimes when I'm with friends who are going through the menopause, I do think that Erkan did me a favour that day, but wow, what a way to do it. A couple of days later my hair also started dropping out! First a clump or two but then just a steady thinning of what thin hair I had already. That lasted for a few weeks and I was really scared I was heading to being bald!   I never saw a doctor at the time, I had no spare cash and no inclination to explain my crappy life to anyone. I threw my wedding ring at him that day, I had never taken it off before but this was the end. He took that too, and I never saw it again.

I remember Erkan saying to me at the time, that my gold and the kid's gold was his to do whatever he liked with!

He had sold my gold, the boys' gold and even my wedding ring to help fund his gambling habit.

It was hard not showing Mum and Dad what was happening, I would keep away from them following the bad times, and that was heart breaking. My Dad was a big man, he was an ex-miner and in his youth was probably a tough guy. But he was getting old, he was retired, he had many back injuries and discs broken and slipped out of place. He had also thought the world of Erkan, he thought he was a good hardworking man, because he had been hardworking during the years we lived in the UK. Dad would still have tackled him, and where on earth would that have ended up?

I stopped talking to Erkan, from that incident onwards. I stopped cooking for him, washing for him. He started sleeping on the sofa when he was there, but he had become absent most of the time, and that suited me.

I continued working in my little shop during the week, and sold things I'd made on a craft fayre at the weekend. I was able to pay the rent for both my shop and house. Cash was difficult for food, but the boys and I got through it. I remember several times, desperately searching through handbags, bags and pockets looking for enough money for a loaf of bread, and they were very cheap in Turkey. I remember a week where I had nothing left after paying both rents. I made up a game with the boys, and we had pancakes and Yorkshire puddings for dinner, all week. It's amazing the things you can do with gravy and jam and fruit if you put your mind to it. I went through that week, hoping that the boys would never remember it!

Erkan then started to appear late at night and shout up to the apartment from the road. He would talk rubbish most of the time; how he had tried his best, how I wasn't helping out. He would say this even though by then I was working in my little shop, working on a craft fayre at the weekends and still undertaking airport transfers whenever I could. He would shout and shout at me. If he ever saw any of the boys' jeans or school trousers hanging on my washing line, which was strung out over the balcony, he would accuse me of having another man living with me. He was just so stupid.

One evening he started banging on the apartment door, I don't know where his key was, but if he had lost it, I was quite pleased. It was late at night and he kept banging, so to save my neighbours any further upset, I opened the door. I was dragged into the kitchen and no words were spoken, but as I was slapped in the face, Kaan walked into the kitchen rubbing sleep from his eyes. The horror of one of my kids finally seeing what was happening was the final straw. I put Kaan back in his bed, hoping he would think he'd had a bad dream. I walked calmly back into the kitchen, Erkan was stood on the kitchen balcony smoking and rubbing his forehead. I took a very sharp vegetable knife out of a drawer and when he turned around, I told him that if he tried to touch me one more time, or if he didn't leave, I would stab him through the heart! Looking back, I was fortunate that he just sniggered and left. But if he had acted differently, I really think I would at that point in my life, have been able to hurt him!

The next day, after the kids were gone, I walked down to the police station. I had a black eye and on the side of my face I had a handprint. I walked into the police station and was asked what the problem was. I told them I wanted to report my husband for abuse, I was planning to divorce him, and I had made that decision when the knife was in my hand the previous evening. I wanted proof of abuse.

First of all, they asked me to take a seat and they left me for over an hour. Once the hour was over, they begrudgingly took some details. When I told them the name of my husband, they knew him. Unbeknown to me, he had fitted some of the air conditioning in the police Station. They then seemed to relax and told me to go home, make friends with Erkan, let him say sorry and get over it! I had been in a very hot police station in a room filled with various thieves, prostitutes, teenagers who had done goodness knew what, and I had just about had my fill. I argued back with the two policemen and told them that, as an English woman living abroad, I would probably be better off just going to the newspapers. Turkey was busy trying to gain access to the European Community, but they were seemingly condoning me being abused? I must have raised my voice as a door in the corridor opened. It was someone with a higher rank, who was wearing a really fancy uniform. He told me I was basically out of order, and what did I think I was shouting at? The policemen who had been dealing with me went out into the corridor and spoke to 'General Admission' or whatever his name was!

They came back and asked me to wait a little longer, they would sort it. I would not give in, I had come this far. An hour later Erkan walked in, he had clearly received a phone call, and I imagine it went something like 'Your wife is here causing a fuss, come and sort her out mate!' Erkan was smirking and said to me 'You won't get anywhere in here'.

This incensed me, and I did indeed feel he was right. I was sitting next to a table with nothing more than 2 telephones sitting on it. Most of the people who had been waiting in the room with me had now gone, there was just a young girl in there with me now, she was a pickpocket, and she was watching this foreigner with great interest.

I had been in the Police station about four hours by now, and I decided to wipe the smile of Erkan's face. I stood up, walked to the table and with one clean sweep of my arm, I cleared the table! I told them to either arrest me, or take my abuse report seriously and take me to the hospital to be checked so I could have a written report! Silence. Deafening silence from everyone, including General Admission, who had popped his head out of his office again to see what the noise was about.

I have to admit that, although I didn't regret it, I was now crapping myself and worried about the boys, but General Admission reappeared, spoke to the policemen and they then asked me outside. One of them said that they had agreed that Erkan could take me to the hospital and get my report! We were now moving into the realms of comedy. This was Erkan, who was not only the man who had left the bloody mark on my face in the first place, but also Erkan the man who didn't even have a driving licence.

After another little fracas during which I explained this to the police, they once again begrudgingly brought a police car around to the front of the police station. I climbed into the back of it, but even as they drove me to the hospital one of them was telling me I'd done the wrong thing. He and his wife often had arguments but they were made up the following day and that's what I should be doing. In reply I said I would give him my number and the next time he 'argued' with his wife she could call me and I'd help her deal with the police. They stopped talking to me then!

I did however get to the hospital, I was examined and all the marks I had were recorded, I was taken back to the police station, gave an official report and walked home with copies of everything.

Mission complete!

Mutha Fucca Yucca

As you read away, you may be tempted to think that all I did when I lived in Turkey was drink. Well I didn't, but like everything else that I did, I drank my fair share, and I did live in Turkey for ten years. I want to tell you about one particular night that was quite an adventure.

I was out drinking with my rep pals, the transfer girls, the top team. It was just before a new season. The Scandinavians were there already but not many Brits. We were actually the oldest bunch of transfer reps ever, and we did sometimes get rude comments at the airport, but we were THE best ever. We all knew our job, we took it seriously, we were professional and polite and very, very good with customers. Some of us had second and third jobs, some had pensions from the UK and some had Turkish husbands or boyfriends. So we were rather an eclectic mix of women who had all become good friends through fate.

I can't place this night very well, I don't know where exactly it should be chronologically. The date isn't important, the night was. I do believe that through the Head Rep, Lynda, we had all been invited to the Tequila Bar. I think the theory being that we could then recommend it to the customers once the season started. It was the top level of a 3 storey building which was one of the busiest nightclubs in Alanya. Now, I for one had never drunk Tequila before. I will never drink it again, and I know I'm not the only one of that group.

We were shown how to drink Tequila, which in our eyes was just too pigging complicated, but we persevered. We weren't paying for these drinks so they flowed, they flowed so well. We all seemed to have 'got the taste' for this. But I have to say it wasn't an attractive scene after a couple of hours. We were no longer elegant. We were a large group of older ladies who should have known better. Some were 'dancing', some were staggering around, some had their heads on the bar and the rest of us were just absolutely smashed!

The time to leave the bar was decided when we just couldn't cope with salt, lick, lemon, glass ritual anymore. The order had gone, we couldn't do it! We had to walk down three steep flights of stairs just to get out. It seemed, if I remember rightly, to be worse than climbing Everest, and we were going down. We hung onto bannisters, we hung onto each other, we hung onto innocent passers-by and we hung onto men who we frightened to death. But we fulfilled the challenge and made it to the ground floor.

Some who lived further away, dragged their sorry asses towards the taxi rank, we knew they got home safe as we were all on the minibus the following week for work. We said very little about this night though.

Incredibly, some had, and I will forever remain impressed that they were able to do it, called boyfriends, husbands or partners and were 'collected'. Actually, I should have said 'swept up' at the door of the nightclub. But 4 or 5 of us all lived in the same direction and we had decided to walk. As foolish as it seems, we were not only always broke, but we were all very tight. We hadn't paid for a single drink, so why spoil a perfectly good night by making our lives easy and climbing into taxis. Ha, not us, we were made of stronger stuff than that.

We set off, laughing and messing about through the bazaar area, past bars and restaurants, and were totally oblivious to how loud we must have been and how ridiculous we must have looked. We were doing well. Not one of us fell down, not one of us lost any shoes, and after about an hour we reached the crossroads where we all normally split up. We said some rather emotional Goodbyes and off we went. From there I had to cross the road, it was by now about 3am so not busy thankfully. I then had to climb quite a steep hill to my apartment block. There was then a large, very heavy metal door to unlock to get into the block. Finally, lots of stairs, and I mean lots. There were two long sets for every floor, and I was on the third floor.

At the time this was happening, my boys were in Kemer with their Nana and Grandad on a little holiday. I love my Mum and Dad, they took the boys on little trips often, it was great for the boys, and I didn't worry as the boys were old enough by then to help Mum and Dad with the language.

I woke up very early the next morning and I really thought I'd picked up some killer death bug. I felt dreadful, as if I had a slipper in my mouth that Gandhi had worn when he walked across India. I was fully dressed, and I had stockings on, as the previous night was a 'big night out' and I'd done the whole best dressed thing. But, my stockings had holes all over them, some of the holes had developed into ladders, it was so attractive, I don't think. I tried getting up, which was when I saw what looked like little knife wounds all over me, my arms, my neck, even my face. Oh my God, I'd been attacked! I got to my bedroom door but as I opened it and was about to step out, I almost took my eye out on the biggest Yucca plant I had ever seen. It was in the bedroom doorway! What the hell?

I had no choice but to drag the Yucca out of the way, so I dragged it across my hallway floor and pushed it into a corner out of the way. I cleared up the mess I'd made on the floor and went into the shower. As I came out of the shower, I looked like I'd had a street fight. I dressed with long sleeves, high necks and baggy pants and that was probably a good thing, as a few minutes later the doorbell chimed. I opened the door to see the landlord's wife standing there.

She asked me if I had heard anything the previous night as she had a few of the tenants saying there had been a commotion in the early hours of the morning. She also pointed to a trail of dirt which seemed to become thinner and thinner up the stairs and ultimately stop almost at my door. Now, as I genuinely had no idea how the Mutha Fucca Yucca that was in the corner behind the open door had found its way into my home, I decided that a full on lie would probably be the best thing. So, I shook my head, put my best 'shocked' look on and totally denied any knowledge of either the commotion or the dirt! Shocking I know, but we have all been in a place like that in our pasts. She smiled, and I knew that she knew. But she carried on by saying that, as it was Saturday it wasn't too bad, because the lady that cleaned the communal areas, ie the stairs, would be there soon anyway, so there would be no extra cost for the clean-up to be paid by anyone. She left and I knew I would never be able to look her in the eye again!

The day rolled by, I felt absolutely dreadful, my head was clearly about to fall off, I felt sick and promised myself several times that I would never drink Tequila again. And I never have. But as the day rolled on, I was getting flashbacks, and I continued to get these for most of the weekend. This is the explanation that I eventually pieced together:

On the previous night, as we were all standing at the crossroads saying our emotional Goodbyes, I hadn't gone straight across the road. For some unfathomable reason, I had headed to a hotel on that very same crossroads, I don't think they were open for business yet. Again for some unfathomable reason, I must have taken a liking for the Yucca, as it was one of several, planted in big pots, in the doorway and surrounding area. And yes, I realised at the time that it was theft. I had gotten hold of the plant and dragged it across the road. Then I had dragged it up the very steep hill. Once through the apartment block door, I then dragged it up every step. I can only begin to imagine the noise that must have made. The plant was way too heavy to carry, so dragging it up three flights of stairs must have taken Herculean strength, but being fired by tequila, I clearly thought that I could do anything!

Whilst undertaking my Herculean task, the f***king plant had, in return for the trip, stabbed, cut and basically tried it's best to mutilate me. It had also lost a little bit of the soil from it's pot on almost every step on the way up.

OK so now what to do? I didn't want something that size living with us. It may well have caused the death of one of the boys. I could hardly just launch it off the balcony onto the rough ground at the side of the apartment block. The chances of being seen doing that were pretty high! OK so I needed to think realistically. I did the only thing that I could do. I invited a couple of unscrupulous friends around. I plied them with drink, and we waited until it was truly dark outside and we couldn't see anyone out on their balconies on my side of the building. I had covered the top of the pot with plastic as I didn't want to get the bill for the stair cleaner, I had gotten away with it once. We carried the bloody dangerous plant back down, but we were prepared. I had previously purchased safety equipment; we all had rubber gloves on!

We carried it down the steps, really quietly apart from the occasional giggle. We carried it down the steep hill, but at the bottom to our horror we saw that the lights in the hotel were on. It was open. Quietly, apart from the occasional pip from passing cars who clearly thought it was a funny sight, we got back across the road. We decided we only had one chance at this, the lights were on but there was no sign of anyone around, so we moved swiftly, yeah right, and dropped the pot containing the killer plant back in the vacant spot between the other killer plants. I pulled the plastic off, and then I pulled out a plastic seaside type bucket and spade from a carrier bag I'd brought along. I placed them on top of the pot, together with a little note saying 'Glad to be back! X'

Gloves were removed and disposed of, conscience was clear. It was no longer plant theft, more like plant rental, and life got back to normal!

The Best Rep?

I needed to make a living. How can this be done in a foreign country with minimal knowledge of the language, no skills I could use, and two small kids in tow? Well, I had English friends who were undertaking holiday transfers and although it didn't pay a huge amount, it was a start. I asked about, and was thankfully given an opportunity with Airtours. On my first trip out I didn't get paid, as I was shadowing a friend, Jackie, who had been doing transfers for a while. My extremely kind next door neighbour offered for her son to look after my boys, so before I went to work, the boys were put to bed and the neighbours son came in to stay with them. Looking back I don't know how I would have gotten through life without the many fantastic Turkish neighbours I had at various times.

A year or so later, I also undertook transfers for Sunworld Ireland, but once again I had great neighbours who would help by looking after the kids, and whilst I look back and wonder what kind of a mother I was, I know I did the best I could and given alternatives I might have done things differently, but I didn't have alternatives.

Sun World Ireland was hard work. We started work at about 11pm on a Saturday evening when we were picked up by Minibus, to be taken to the hotel in Mahmutlar, a 20 minute drive away, where all the Irish were staying. This shift was a killer, we took guests to the airport, a two hour drive, and once they were checked in we had to sit and wait until the plane took off. We would then drive back in a minibus to Alanya, get home, have a shower and something to eat, and then head back to the office to put all the arrivals paperwork together. Then it was a minibus back to the airport to collect the arrivals, and back to the hotel. Finally, before we all collapsed, we were given food by the hotel, normally soup or a pizza, and finally we would get home about 2am on Monday morning. All this to earn £25!

Imagine if you can, a hotel full of Irish guests being collected at midnight; 8 coach loads! All of them would be sitting at, or near, the hotel bar. Are you getting the picture? The coaches, and sometimes a minibus, would all queue up the hillside on the road outside the hotel. Each bus had a number, the reps were positioned from the hotel doorway out of the gate and up to the top of the road, in an attempt to get everyone on the correct bus so we knew we had collected everyone!

First hurdle, understanding some of the accents when they gave their names to the rep in the hotel doorway, in return we gave them their coach number then ushered them out of the doorway out of the gateway and onto the pavement where the next rep would send them up the hill towards the correct coach. Sounds easy yes? Ah but these people were still in holiday mood, no rush, wanting to have their last chat with friends they had made during their stay, girls all having a last minute snog with the guys they had hooked up with. A last minute smoke. No interest in collecting their suitcases whatsoever and certainly no interest in getting onto their coach!

As a rep, when everyone had gotten onto their coaches I would climb onto my coach and start counting. Never, and I mean never, would you have the right number or the right families, 10 minutes was then spent with the reps wandering up and down the hill looking for specific people only to find them on another coach. Their excuse for being on the wrong coach?. Well, they wanted to sit with friends of course. There was always at least one suitcase left in the hotel foyer so the owner had to be found so they could go get their case. The girls had to be dragged, normally crying as they were pulled from the 'love of their lives' but little did they know that these same guys would be there every week having girls pulled off them! All this done, you might finally pull away from the hotel. You might get drunks, people who had not taken their meds and were incredibly difficult to deal with. People who were physically ill during the transfer as they had too much to drink. Fights were a regular occurrence as well, I once remember, when we were waiting for arrivals, that two middle aged women, came thundering out of the arrivals terminal, absolutely ripping into each other, gold was being ripped off their necks, clothes torn and language to make your hair curl. But by the time we arrived at the resort they were best friends and loved each other again.

I want to tell you about a particular night which proves you really, really should never upset your rep! At this point, I'd been living in Turkey for a couple of years, and had a passable amount of Turkish. My coach that evening, was No 8 which was the top of the queue right at the top of the hill, so the furthest away from the hotel gate.

The hotel was empty, everyone on their coaches, no unclaimed baggage, no crying girls so should be good to go. I climbed onto my coach and walked to the back counting. Not good, one missing! So, I walked back to the front of the coach to start counting again in case I'd made a mistake. Nope, still one missing, so once again I walked towards the back counting and asking if anyone had one member of their group missing, toilet visit etc. Nope, and no one was offering up any useful information. Back at the front of the bus, the driver, who had been standing outside on the pavement, tells me there were two girls jumping on and off the coach at the back door, sharing a cigarette. 'OK' says I, 'close the back door.' He tells me that there is still one of the girls on the pavement. 'That's OK' I say, she'll soon put her cigarette out and get on board.

The door is closed, and yes she ran to the front and climbed on board. As she walks to the back of the coach, I hear mutterings, 'fat hitler rep' 'think they are bloody clever' etc etc.

We pull away from the hotel, the last of the coaches to leave, and I break into my rep persona, on the microphone asking that everyone make sure they have their passport and tickets, explaining that we will be having a comfort break about an hour later when we are halfway to the airport.

We had almost left the resort and I was sitting completing paperwork when one of these two girls sat down next to me, in fact she sat heavily on my bag, I later discovered she had broken a pair of sunglasses. Her words; 'I need a piss.' 'mmmm' says I, 'sorry but you will have to wait until we arrive at the comfort stop, we are already running late.' Then the other girl, who has come forward, states she 'needs a piss' as well! I tell them both I will see what I can do.

They return to their seats and in my best Turkish I ask the driver to stop at the Total Fuel Station just outside the resort, he tries to tell me that the Total is a horrible garage but just a mile or so past there is a nice clean Shell Garage. I tell him I know, and I do know, as I once had the misfortune to stop at a Total garage once, and they have the old fashioned open hole style toilets. Stinky, dirty and normally only used by truck drivers and farmers. I urged the driver to stop where I ask.

A few minutes later, we pull into the garage, I go to rep persona and ask everyone else to stay on the coach. The two girls jump off, slightly drunk and laughing and joking. I explain in my best rep voice that as they can't wait, this is the only other stop available, and that the toilets won't be up to standard!

'Ha, ha', they both say, 'we can piss anywhere'. Strangely enough I can believe that! I head towards the toilet door, but I strategically stop at least 2 meters away. As the 'ladies' get to the door, I hear them both start retching. I was getting a little sample of the awful stench where I was standing, so could only begin to imagine! I heard then cursing and retching, one of them had jeans on, she had been poured into them and I could hear her say that she couldn't get her jeans down and hold her nose at the same time ! The other was swearing and saying that she had wet her pants trying to pee over the hole. I really was enjoying their plight by now. Very shortly after they both exited the toilet and one still had her jeans down round her knees, she had peed all over hers too.

As they exited the toilet I reminded them that I had told them how bad the toilets were, but as they weren't inclined to wait, I'd had no choice. To make things even more embarrassing, the driver then offered them some old cloths from the baggage hold of his coach to sit on so his seats wouldn't be soiled. The rest of the journey they were like little lambs, and the driver, Mustafa, said he would now never ever get on my wrong side. 2 minutes down the road we sped past the Shell Garage where there were beautifully clean, nicely smelling European style toilets! Ahhh Karma is a bitch at times.

Moral ….. be nice to your rep!

The Holidays

There were two very rare occasions when I had both the time and the finances to afford very short holidays for the boys and myself. On both occasions I called in favours I had due from the owner of the rent-a-car firm I had an arrangement with. A small car was provided for me for three days.

So, without telling the boys I packed a couple of bags and on the last day of school before the long school holidays I headed out to collect them from school. They were amused, not sure what was going on but more than willing to wait and see. I'd brought them a change of clothes and they changed in the back of the car, we headed to their favourite kebab shop and I got them something to eat and when back in the car, I asked 'OK boys, left or right'? A combined 'What'? from the rear of the car. Again I asked, smiling and of course, one said left, the other said right

We were parked on the main street in Alanya. Anyone who has been there will probably know where the statue of Ataturk is, anyone else, well, the main street is quite literally a long reasonably straight road, that runs right through Alanya. One way would take you towards Antalya and ultimately north, the opposite way ultimately towards Syria. The boys had previously been to places in both directions, we had had holidays from the UK to Marmaris and Bodrum, they'd visited Kusadasi, and they had been the other way, to Anamur, Osmaniye, and to Carole Annes's engagement party in Erzin.

I gave them another chance left or right? And the decision was made, right it was! I turned the car and off we headed towards Antalya and the North. The boys chatted and laughed, and it was a good time in the car. It was a long journey, I'd done it before, but this time the company I had was great fun. We laughed, we, well they, argued a little. We stopped at the great comfort stops that are located along the main routes in Turkey. I was unsure where we were actually going, my thought had been to stop when I was too tired to drive anymore! Fehiye, Marmaris maybe Bodrum, Kusadasi? We drove past Antalya and up over the Taurus mountains, an easy road to drive on, and hours sped by as we travelled along, it had been a lovely hot day, but I hadn't picked the boys up until after school so it was a late start. It was dark and the boys were napping in the rear of the car. I saw the sign for Marmaris and thought that should be the final destination. It felt good to just 'up and go' without planning. We pulled up in front of a hotel in the early hours of the morning, I asked if there were any rooms and there was, the hotel was in a great place, across the road was a five minute walk down to the path that ran along the beachfront towards the marina and bazaar area.

We checked in, unloaded the bags and I parked the car up. We headed to our room and within a few short minutes we were all fast asleep. Our holiday had begun! I remember waking and the room was still dark, the boys and I were all in the massive king size bed, not sure why as there were two beds in the room, but I wasn't complaining. I was woken up by one of them moaning about being hungry. I was horrified but amused at the same time when I checked the time, and realised that we had slept the whole of the day and it was 8.30pm! We got up, showered and headed out, I was determined to give the boys a good time and it wasn't very often I had 'money to burn'! We had something to eat and I told them they could choose something new to wear. Aslan picked the strangest thing... it was a shirt, like a bowling type shirt and it had flames around the bottom, he also asked for a bandana to tie around his head, and that remained firmly around his head every minute he was awake and not in water of some description. Kaan, on seeing Aslan's new attire, chose the same! I was happy, they were loving this!   As we walked back to the hotel, I asked the boys what they wanted to do during the days we were here. A boat trip was the united reply They had been on boat trips millions of times over the last couple of years, I really thought they would have gone for the pool as a choice as we didn't get the chance to swim in a pool very often. But no, boat trip it was.

As we walked back, we reached the marina where all the tourist boats were moored up. Guys stood in front of their boats trying to attract potential customers. The boys were drawn to the smallest of the boats and as the guys in front started talking to me in English, the boys started speaking to them in Turkish. We made a deal, it seemed that the boys wanted to go on the boat both days we would be in Marmaris, so I said OK.

The following morning, we got up early, had breakfast in the hotel and headed out to our boat for the day. It was much smaller than the boats we normally went on and most of the other customers, although there weren't a lot, were Turkish. The boat stopped about twenty minutes later for a swim break. The boys and I were ready and in we all jumped! Oh my lord, it was absolutely freezing! It was mid-July in Turkey, we had been swimming in the sea off Alanya for weeks, and that was like being in a nice warm bath! I climbed back on board, with the speed and dexterity of a gazelle! OK, so I clambered onboard in the most inelegant way ever but wowser it was cold! I realised that we were much further North and that was the first and last time I would jump in the sea off Marmaris. The boys, however, were made of stronger stuff than me and they, pardon the pun, took to it like ducks to water!

The day was good, the guys on the boat were good fun, they let the boys fish with them, help cook the fish and they chatted as all Turks did with my sons. Wanting to know all about them, how they were there, where they came from, what the UK was like. We travelled along the coast to a spot which was known to be lucky and our boat took it's turn to queue up to get close enough to throw money over the side to make a wish. At the next stopping point, the boys had developed such a good relationship with the crew that they were let into a secret. As the customers were all dipping their toes in or swimming or sunbathing, the crew pulled out a little zodiac inflatable boat, and they told the boys they could go with them if I gave my permission, which I happily did. They zipped off and were gone about 30 minutes.

When they arrived back, the boys were laughing, but wouldn't say anything to me until we were back at the marina in Marmaris and walking back towards the hotel. 'OK where did you go'? Their reply was nothing like I expected, they explained that they had gone back to the 'lucky place' and the crew from the boat had dived in and collected the money that were peoples wishes. They made a decent haul apparently, and even gave Aslan and Kaan some 'pocket money'. The moral of that is quite clear!

The following day was pretty much the same routine, up, breakfast and down to the boat. Another day of swimming for the boys, topping my tan up for me and listening to the Turkish customers freak out when a pod of dolphins decided to swim along side the boat! Not the first time I'd seen other guests freak out thinking we were being surrounded by sharks!

Before lunch Aslan came on board all excited about finding an abandoned anchor whilst he was swimming and snorkelling! If this was right then he was in for making some more cash as they weren't cheap things to buy! He told the same crew who had given him 'lucky money' the previous day and he went on and on and on about it until a couple of them agreed to have a look after lunch. He was so excited. True to their word, after lunch

96

had been eaten and cleared away, a couple of the crew got Aslan into the little zodiac and they were off. About 30 minutes later, they were back, and the crew were laughing, but Aslan wasn't. They had reached the spot Aslan thought was right, gone in together and found the anchor, they then found the chain fastened to it and traced it to another tourist boat that had drifted quite a way from the anchor!

Aslan went quiet about that anchor, but Kaan still brings the subject up when they are 'arguing' at dinner!

We headed back to Alanya the following morning, we had had a wonderful fun filled few days, we didn't need to spend a lot, but boy we packed in a lot of laughter, some good food and a lot of very fond memories.

The second of our two holidays was really a combination of getting in the car and turning left instead of right, and a trip to Carole-Anne and Yusuf's engagement party. During the weekend we went to the party though, I decided to introduce the boys to real culture and I took them into Hatay before we went home. I took them inside St Peter's church, one of the first Christian churches ever. As kids do, they didn't think very much to that, but they did like the food!

An update on Carole-Anne: She is now married to a Scot called Brian. Yusuf continued to have engagement parties, Carole-Anne was number one, but Yusuf had 4 more! Clearly, as nice as he was, he had turned into a serial fiancée!

During the corona virus lockdown, Carole-Anne and her husband created Coronaoke on Facebook, it was an initial attempt at keeping in touch during lockdown, but became a unique approach to opening a support network. Carole-Anne is involved in health, welfare and well-being for a charity called

Turning Point Scotland. Last time I looked Coronaoke had over 17,000 members!

Fakes anyone?

During my time as a rep/guide I met many unusual people from all over the UK. Mainly nice happy people, they were on their holidays afterall! During one excursion, I was guiding a trip from Alanya so a shorter day for me as we only needed to collect the guests from their various hotels in Alanya and then to a great place called Side, about an hour's drive away. I met a fun lady called Val. Val was on holiday with her two daughters, and as well as having a great week in a nice hotel in Alanya they were on a mission ! I had an Isuzu bus, so probably 20 to 25 guests, and one of my two favourite drivers. A guy called Kismet.

During the journey I did my normal guide 'bit' explaining all about Side, what we would be seeing when we arrived, and the route we would take once in the town. I explained what we were passing, as lots of people hadn't seen the sesame pyramids, they'd only seen sesame on their burger bun, or they hadn't seen cotton growing. Depending what time of year it was, and depending which driver I had, we would sometimes stop the bus and the driver would jump off, hop the ditch or hedge into the field, and bring a stem back with cotton growing on it. The kids, and sometimes the adults, were truly fascinated! I also explained that there was a restaurant we recommended, and that after we had seen Apollo's temple in the harbour area, everyone was free to roam and shop for a couple of hours before meeting up for the journey back to their hotels.

Side has an Amphitheatre at the top of a peninsula which is about 1 mile long and ¼ mile wide. Past the theatre the road down the hill is full of shops and restaurants, and once at the bottom there is the harbour. Walk along the harbour front and a wonderful surprise is waiting. The Temple of Apollo, which consists of five remaining columns from a temple which in its time must have been one of the most glorious sites in Anatolia. If you chose, you can walk back to the Amphitheatre at the top of Side, round the coastal path alongside the beach. A truly wonderful day out.

On this particular day, we arrived in Side, and, from the car park where the bus stopped we queued to get on the little 'train' that was used to ferry tourists into town. The drive went through Roman ruins, all the remains of tiny shops, past the remains of the market places, and under the archway with Vespasian's statue. The view from here is of the Amphitheatre, and it never ceased to amaze me at it's grandeur.

Once we were off the train and wandering down into town, Val approached me and asked if I knew of any handbag shops. I knew lots of shops but it depended what she wanted. She explained that she and her daughters wanted to buy 'a few' handbags. I told her I had a friend called Apo with a very nice, very large shop down at the bottom of town.

Now, any decent rep or guide worth their salt will try and eke out their earnings with commissions from shop keepers and restaurants. Even if it consists of just free meals or drinks. I was no different. But when I was taking people shopping I always explained that I had 'my shops' where I could barter for them and get good prices, and ensure that they didn't get ripped off, but if they saw something or wanted to buy from somewhere that I didn't know, I would happily help them out.

Val was happy to have a look at Apo's shop and we agreed that in the 'free time' period we would go have a look together. The group walked through the streets, and we eventually got to the restaurant. There was a great little boutique under the restaurant and that was our first call. The guys in there knew me well, they had introduced themselves to me the year before when I first started guiding excursions. The customers entered the shop and the owners, as they always did, handed me an empty shop carrier bag. We had started our 'business' relationship with them telling me that I could take anything I liked from their store, whenever I brought customers in. At the same time they would always make sure that my 'guests' got a good fair price. I found it difficult to just pick things up! But during my first year guiding I took the boys to Side over the weekend when I wasn't working so they could see what I talked about when I got home. That day was truly a nice day. We got to the restaurant I used when guiding, and they wouldn't take any money for our meals. We were then called downstairs into the shop and the owners filled two carrier bags with items the boys indicated they liked! I was wowed, we went down to the harbour and the boys were each given a watch by the guy who sold all the 'fake' watches that the guests walked past on our route. We were all blown away, and I never asked for, or expected any of this.

After the shop owners had seen my boys, they would ensure that I was given items to fit them both every single time I took customers to their shop. Sometimes I was there twice a week. They filled up the carrier bag I was given when I walked into the shop. I never asked, but neither did I feel guilty as I knew my guests were getting good prices as the shop owner wanted me to go back week after week. Volume seemed to be the key. We all won.

Anyhow, after our meal, Val, myself and her daughters went into Apo's shop. We sat, and, as he always did, Apo offered drinks and brought these out with plates of fruit. Val clearly knew what she wanted, and during the conversations it turned out that she and her daughters had been travelling backwards and forwards to Turkey often over the past couple of years. Each time they took suitcases full of handbags home to London with them. It turned out that they were having houseparties, like

101

the good old Tupperware parties. They would invite ladies who knew the bags they were buying were fake, and they would sell them at a massive profit, but much cheaper than the real thing, so providing that the quality was good, the ladies didn't mind! Val knew the sort of quality she wanted, she knew the styles, the zips, the studs on the bottom, the smallest details had to be right!

Living out there, I had a few fake bags, mainly given to me when I was guiding, but I just knew what I liked, so picked a nice style or colour! I'd never really thought about them in such detail.

Val and her daughters spent the next couple of hours, checking, choosing and wandering around the shop. Pretty soon, a selection of handbags, purses, belts and a couple of pairs of shoes were piled high on a table. With my help, Val and Apo came up with a price. All was agreed, handshakes were done. It was a large amount of money, as Val's idea of a few handbags was far different from my idea of a few! I knew Apo had a car and that he regularly travelled to Alanya, so I asked if he could bag everything up and take them to the hotel Val was staying at, to save us the agony of ferrying them all back up the hill and onto the coach. He happily agreed. The money was paid, and we left the shop.

Val and I agreed to have a drink later.

That evening, I was sitting with Val, chatting about how she was making money from the bags. She told me she had spoken to UK Trading Standards and was told by them that it was hard to stop people doing what Val was doing. She bought different brands, and in order to take her to court, a representative from each company needed to check the bag and categorically state it wasn't a 'Louis Vitton' or a 'Prada' or a 'Chanel' or a 'Gucci' etc.

So by buying various brands, and due to the fact that in the grand scale of things Val wasn't selling massive amounts and she was selling from people's houses, rather than in public on markets or car boots, she was able to stay under the wire.

She asked me if there was any way that I could find somewhere to buy the same quality bags at cheaper prices. She was very happy with the bags she'd bought from Apo and wanted more of the same, but would love to get even cheaper prices. This was something very new to me, but as always I said I'd see what I could do. Val had another 4 or 5 days before her holidays was over so, the following day, I spoke to a friend of mind with a bag shop in Alanya.

I found out that most of the handbags sold at the resorts were made in Istanbul, which wasn't really a surprise. My friend gave me a couple of phone numbers but I didn't think my Turkish would be good enough on the phone. It wasn't bad, but without the body language, facial expressions and a little pantomime it was easy to get mixed up. I asked my friend Huseyin to help me out and he was happy to. Following a number of conversations (the guys in Istanbul were very wary, as they didn't have a clue who I was) I discovered that although Val had been given a really good price by Apo, she had spent in excess of £1000 that day!

I arranged to meet Val and I was able to tell her that I believed I could buy bags for her in Istanbul and save her £15 to £20 per bag, depending on which ones she wanted and how many.

Before she left for the UK, Val and I had arranged to buy several thousand pounds worth of bags. She had sat with her daughters, made a lot of phone calls back to the UK to customers, and they came up with an extensive list of brands, bag names and numbers. Then the plan all went a bit pear shaped, as the only way we could buy at this price was to collect them!

Could I do it? Dare I do it? Val had offered me a nice amount of cash if I could sort it. When we had discussed it, she'd said she would happily pay for the hire of a car, all my fuel and overnight expenses, as the drive to Istanbul was at least 12 hours each way.

Scared, but not wanting to turn down such a good opportunity, I agreed. The bags would be available with just two day's notice. I told Val I could get them from Istanbul to Alanya, but the next issue was getting them back to the UK. Val said she would arrange for her and her daughters to come back for a week's holiday, and that they would take them back to the UK. If the volume meant two trips, they would make two trips. She was still able to make money!

Val admitted to me that she was selling the fakes for up to £300 depending what they were. I was shocked, but then she went on to explain that the ladies buying her bags knew they were fakes, and would only buy them if the quality was spot on. They were happy to pay that price for a bag, that if it had been real would retail for thousands!

Over the following few weeks, all was set in motion. Val booked to come back with the girls in a few weeks time. She was very trusting, and forwarded a considerable amount of money to me for the bags and my expenses. I arranged for the call to be made to make sure the bags would be ordered and ready, and I hired a car. A little white Ford Fiesta.

The day arrived and I set off, I'd hidden the money in the car, I fuelled up and started the long drive, it was very early but I really didn't want to arrive too late in Istanbul. The initial part of the drive was easy enough, I'd driven to Antalya often enough, I'd driven to Marmaris with the boys before, and it would be worth it.

Stopping often at the great service stations that coaches stop at in Turkey, I made good progress. I have to say, the best part of the drive was near Afyon as the Sunflowers were almost ready to be harvested. I drove down very long, very straight roads with towering Sunflowers on both sides of the road, for absolutely miles. I so regret that I didn't have a camera with me back then!

As I started to get near to Istanbul the knots in my stomach became hard, I was heading for a region of Istanbul called Lale which I was told was an industrial area.

I didn't have Sat Nav, it wasn't used then, I had a map and I was following roadsigns! The odds were that I probably shouldn't have found where I was going, but I did. To this day I am always astounded that I did it, especially when I have re-visited Istanbul and remember how busy the place is. But I did!

I did at least find Lale and a massive fuel station, which I thought was far enough into Istanbul. In other words I chickened! I really was starting to lose my nerve and the people on the roads weren't particularly friendly. As my number plates clearly showed that I wasn't from Istanbul, they would shout and pip me whenever I hesitated. I called the man I was buying the handbags from, and he happily agreed to come meet me so I could follow him. It wasn't until I was safely back in Alanya the following day that I realised how dangerous, in fact how stupid, what I was doing at that moment actually was! But I followed this guy to a car park outside an apartment block. I followed him into the building and it was evident, that every apartment was a factory. Inside, the noise of sewing machines and other equipment was humming away. The second floor was eye opening. The 'apartment' we walked into was full of men sitting at sewing machines and I could see 'Gucci' everywhere.

I was shown to a room in the apartment where bags, and boxes of flat-packed bags, were neatly stacked. This was what I was there for. It felt like I was in another really bad movie! It was late in the day, and now I slightly panicked, because if I loaded the car up and then parked outside a hotel for the night, the chances were, the car and everything in it would be gone the next day. We arranged for me to go back the following morning to collect the merchandise. I was directed to local hotels and I picked one and checked in. The money I had been given to pay for the bags was now in the bottom of my handbag being held very tightly!

The hotel seemed OK, it was clean enough and not too expensive, and as I'd been driving a very long time I was incredibly tired. I went to the Lokanta that was a couple of doors down from the hotel to have something to eat. And be stared at! Then I went back to my hotel room and unpacked the small amount of overnight things I'd brought. Not sure why, maybe I'd seen too many movies, but once I'd locked the door I put a chair back underneath the door handle, it was then not possible to open the door even with a key. I lay down and went to sleep. I was woken through the night with noises out in the corridor, so many people coming and going, for hours. I realised at some point that this was probably a hotel used by the local ladies of the night! Checked the chair was still propped under the door handle and then I napped really badly the rest of the night.

The following morning I was up, really quickly, showered and without any thought to a coffee, never mind breakfast, I was off. I arrived to collect my bags, checked them all against my list and paid. It was a great relief to give the money over, and then I was off! The little car was absolutely stuffed full of my swag. The boot, well it was a hatchback so the space behind the back seat, the back seat, the floor of the back seat and the front seat and the floor of the passenger front seat. Stuffed! I hadn't really given much thought to the room all this would take! But now I had given myself another headache. Stopping for fuel wasn't an issue, as way back then petrol was served for you and payment was done at the pump, without leaving the side of your car. But stopping for a drink, food or even to grab a take-out coffee was a little more difficult, as it was impossible for anyone walking past my car not to see what I had. I really didn't want someone taking a chance and putting a brick through the window and grabbing what they could!

So, I drove from Istanbul without stopping for a pee, a drink or food! But I got back to Alanya late that night, unloaded the car, peed, drank, ate and collapsed into bed for the best night's sleep ever.

The story doesn't end there though. When Val gave me the name of the hotel they had booked into so that I could meet her and deliver the bags, I didn't recognise the name. It turned out to be in Bodrum and not Alanya. That's a five hour drive away! Val said she thought they were nearby!

Another long drive But that time I got a much bigger car and I didn't go alone…. But that's another story!

To this day I struggle to believe I did this, but it shows, I think, how much a woman can do when it comes to feeding and looking after her family. Wouldn't do it again though!

Just Nipping Down The Road!

I just thought I should end the handbag story. I know you are all sitting on the edge of your chairs, waiting to hear if they got to the UK

Well Val booked her hotel to come back for them, after I had done my own version of Death Race 2000 to Istanbul and back to collect them. But, instead of booking a hotel in Alanya, she somehow managed to book her hotel in a completely different resort! Not one just down the road. No, she booked a hotel in Gumbet, which is very close to Bodrum for anyone who knows that part of the Turkish coast. A good 5, maybe 6 hours drive away. When I found out, I was not only surprised, but I was a bit scared. I really couldn't face driving for hours again on my own with thousands of pounds of handbags as company. Another run over the Taurus mountains that surround Alanya, lots of empty roads, not being able to stop for a pee or a drink again! It looked like I was wimping out, but I had gotten the bloody things this far. My apartment was full of them!

That weekend, while I was at work in my 'other' job as a transfer rep for Airtours, I was sitting on one of the buses waiting for the arrival of our flight. Each week all the reps would take their bus to the airport with their departing guests, then we would hang about until the plane had landed and the new arriving guests came out of the terminal for us to take back to Alanya. During the wait, I would normally go sit on one of the buses with other reps and drivers. We had a laugh most weeks. There was a café outside the terminal for us all but none of us had any money, so we would make our own entertainment and take drinks with us.

On this particular occasion, most of the flights for Airtours were during the night, which was good really because hanging around in our polyester uniforms in the intense heat wasn't easy at the best of times. I was sitting on one of the Isuzu buses and Kismet, Ahmet and myself were dreaming about having our tour company and what we would and wouldn't do. Anyhow during the conversation I mentioned the handbags, they already knew I'd been to Istanbul to collect them, which they found amazing, but they did tell me I could have been murdered! Thanks guys! During the conversation, Kismet said if he could get someone to cover any runs he had, he would drive up to Bodrum with me. He had a friend called Yusuf working up there. Yusuf, Kismet and Ahmet all grew up in the same place, but due to work they hadn't seen each other for years. That was Ok with me, I'd known Kismet for a couple of years and he was a good guy. So, it was all put in place, he helped me hire a bigger car, well a Citroen Berlingo which had lots of space to put the bags, and I arranged with Val when we would be there. All sorted

On the day of travel we set off early and Kismet drove all the way. I didn't complain, and I think he was worried about being with a woman driver. The Turks were odd with women drivers. A friend of mine, Lynda once asked me if I'd noticed being stared at when I was driving around Alanya, especially stopped at traffic lights. I had, but I just put it down to the fact that the car I was using was out of the ordinary. Most of the cars you saw back then were Tofas cars, which were used like a uniform by the Turks. I was normally in a bright red Ford Fiesta, and Lynda drove a white mini bus. Lynda pointed out that actually we were being stared at because we were, and I mean this, the only women drivers in Alanya at that time! Imagine it, the 21st century was upon us and in a city as big as Alanya, we were the only women driving cars!

Anyway, Kismet drove, and we were able to stop at the services, taking it in turns to go get a drink and use the toilets etc. The journey went well.

It had been a long time since I was in Bodrum, it brought back a mixture of memories, good and bad, especially when we drove along the harbour road and past the Amca bar where I had first met Erkan. But that was another lifetime ago. We had to drive through Bodrum to get to the next resort called Gumbet. The last time I had been to Bodrum, there were several miles of scrub land between the two resorts, but now they just merged and there was no knowing which was which.

We arrived at Val's hotel, we had a laugh about it being just down the road. Yeah right! I really liked Val and her daughters, they were just naturally nice people, and I would have done anything to help her out. The bags were unloaded and I have no idea how they got them all home to the UK, but they were confident they wouldn't have any problems. My part was played out. Val had once again paid for the car and the fuel and had sorted out a room for me.

Later I learned that, although Val and her daughters had a large quantity of flat packed bags, they got through customs with no trouble. This was almost 20 years ago. I can only assume that the customs and airport security weren't as good, or on the ball as they are now. An Airtours rep friend of mine travelled home about three times during that same year for long weekends, each time with a suitcase containing nothing more than cartons of cigarettes. She was never stopped once.

We all had dinner together that evening. Kismet had spoken to his friend Yusuf, and we had arranged to meet him and his girlfriend later in the evening. Val and her daughters declined, they wanted to look through their bags and start packing them away. Kismet and I headed out and met up with Yusuf, whose English was very good, and Carole-Anne his lovely girlfriend, a Scot with a wonderful accent. It made me wonder if Yusuf understood everything she was saying sometimes, but they were a really nice couple that fit together really well. Carole-Anne was an Airtours rep, and had met Yusuf as he was her regular bus driver. We had a fun night in a nightclub that they knew well, and we all promised to keep in contact. Lots of times this happens but you never speak to people again. In this case we did.

The following day, Kismet and I started homeward bound, said bye to Val and the girls and I was really happy that the bags were a memory now! I knew if Val got them home, that she would make a financial killing, and I'd done OK out of it. But do it again?…. Mmmm doubt it!

Life went on in Alanya for the next few months. The season was coming to an end and the whole city was in wind-down mode when I received a phone call from Carole-Anne. She was going to Erzin to visit Yusuf's family and wanted to see me on the way, Yusuf had gone home a few weeks earlier, but Carole-Anne still had guests to deal with so couldn't travel with him. Carole-Anne and I devised a plan that she should use one of the many coach companies to get to Alanya. Travelling on these was pretty comfortable as the seats were comfy and they had stewards on board running up and down with drinks and food. They stopped frequently, and provided you didn't sit near anyone with smelly feet, it was all good. The companies tried very hard not to seat a man next to a lone woman, so invariably, and it always happened to me, travelling as a lone female meant you had an empty seat next to you.

Carole-Ann would come to Alanya and stay with me for a few days, meet the boys and I could show her around the town.

Yusuf would drive from Erzin to collect her, and if he wanted to, he could stay a day or so as well. Kismet had left the resort as the season was at an end, so he would see Yusuf and Carole-Ann when they got back to Erzin.

I met Carole-Ann at the bus station and it was like meeting an old friend, we had a day and night and the boys and I showed her around Alanya. We talked, laughed and had fun. Yusuf turned up and he and the boys got on well. The following day they left to go to Erzin and once again life went back to normal. I was by then working hard in the summer months, but during the winter months I did anything I could, anywhere. Winter work was sketchy. I even worked a short while in a local restaurant, a typically Turkish Lokanta restaurant which was located next to the site of the massive Friday market, and they stayed open all year.

The season's end was a worrying time for everyone, I was no different.

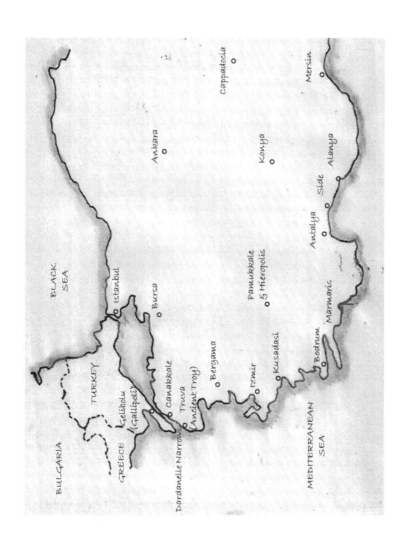

Sunflower Tours

Sunflower Tours is a great name for a tour business that lasted no longer than a few months. Sunflower tours came into being when I was sitting killing time in the car park of Antalya airport waiting for another Airtours flight to arrive with my two favourite bus drivers, Kismet and Ahmet, and a great Turkish guide called Ozzie..

We had been dreaming of having our own business, day dreaming, for a while, but this particular evening, things started turning serious. 'Why couldn't we do things ourselves?' 'We had drivers, we had the best guide' (everyone loved Ozzie) and 'someone English doing Admin, marketing, PR?' Well why couldn't we?

We became determined to see if it was indeed possible, and we all decided to meet one evening when none of us were working to see what we could come up with. Sounded easy eh? Well we all got together several times, maps, brochures, a lot of Ozzie's files plus two excited boys of mine trying to find out what we were planning.

We put a few routes together, routes that would last 7 to 10 days depending which route was to be followed. The drivers knew the routes and timings, Ozzie knew where we should head to show people things that weren't normally on regular tours. I learned so much. My part was initially to see what we could do to find suitable hotels that would deal with us. I also needed to look into what would be needed in the form of licences, and to generally find out what was needed to make us legal. Kismet and Ahmet owned the buses they drove, which was good as a lot of the drivers rented, and which wouldn't have worked. OK, so maybe not so easy, but we were all really determined to see if this dream could be made into a reality.

We all decided that Bergama (Pergamon) should be included. Its on the coast near Izmir, known as the city of firsts. It is the place where the First use of Parchment for writing was recorded. It is the site of one of the First 7 churches of early Christianity, it had the First Theatre with a wooden stage and the First Trade Union, amongst other firsts. You should read up about if you have an interest in Turkey or Roman and Byzantine history.

We wanted to include Canakkale on the Dardanelle straits, which is a gateway to the WW1 Gallipoli battle grounds known as Gelibolu in Turkey. 500,000 soldiers lost their lives in Gallipoli, Turks and Allied soldiers alike.

From Canakkale it's also possible to visit the site of Troy. Homer immortalised Troy in his stories of Hector, Paris and the beautiful Helen. Archeologists have discovered at least 9 separate periods of settlement there, and a symbolic huge wooden trojan horse marks the legendary war.

One of the routes had a stop in Istanbul, but in Bursa, a beautiful part of the region, not in the normal tourist spots.

Ankara was on the list as the political centre of Turkey, with many unusual buildings and the Anitkabir, the hilltop mausoleum of Mustafa Kemal Ataturk, modern Turkey's first president who declared Ankara the capital of Turkey in 1923.

Pamukkale was added, which is also a fabulous place to visit, where mineral rich water flows down the mountain side causing terraces with small white pools. Pamukkale means cotton castle. It shares it's site with Hierapolis, an ancient Roman spa city. There is still an ancient pool that you can swim in, which has submerged antique columns laying on the bottom.

Cappadocia was a must. It is an amazing place, a world heritage site, full of fairy-like chimney structures, Bronze age homes carved into valley walls by troglodytes and which were later used by refugee Christians. There are open air museums and deep caves that can be toured. Most amazing of all are the balloon rides over the top, undertaken early in the morning.

The last must visit place on our list was Konya where the Sufi whirling Dervishes of the Mevlevi order performed.

Then back to Antalya!

The first step, we thought, was to follow this route, check out the hotels and see if they would be prepared to make formal contracts with us. At the same time a web site was being created by another friend, and I had started making enquiries about licences/permits etc. It was really starting.

Ozzie couldn't spare time off work, but Kismet, Ahmet and myself planned to 'do' the route and we surely did. We set off, and in one week we covered every stop on our planned itinerary. I spoke to hoteliers and most were happy to deal with us, only the busy places where tourists regularly visited, ie Pamukkale and Cappadocia, were a little hesitant as they clearly didn't need the extra business. But on the whole, we managed to complete our task favourably. I have to say, travelling with two very funny guys who wouldn't let me drive at all was interesting to say the least. They stopped as we were driving through Sunflower fields and cut the head off a flower and spent an hour in the car eating the seeds! They stopped at service stations and then would pull up under the constant flow of water that the stations left running for people to wash their cars down. And every bloody time they would catch me by pulling under the shower then automatically opening the window where I was sitting, haha! The first time was funny, the second and third not so funny, so I started getting out before they showered the car which made them laugh.

I saw places I never knew existed. I wanted to share all of them with adventurous tourists, and when we arrived back in Alanya I was excited and ready to take this further. I apologise if I bore you with the descriptions of the places, but I love Turkey and always will, the real people and the real places can be spectacular. Turkey is so much more than sunshine, sunbeds and shopkeepers dragging you into their shops.

As is the way with Turks, there are few secrets, and shortly after our tour was finished, and to be honest I can't really remember how it came about but I was offered the chance to go to Erzin and meet up with a travel company about renting the licence I needed from them. It all happened really quickly and next thing I knew, I was driving to Erzin with Yusuf. We went to the offices of the Travel Company, and they turned out to be really, really religious people. It was a family business, nice people but I felt a little uncomfortable because I didn't have my head covered Fortunately I was wearing jeans and a baggy long sleeved high neck top. These guys were great, and they said they would happily rent their name to me for a very small amount, so I would be covered by their licence. To be fair, I didn't fully understand the legalities, but intended learning more before I took them up on their kind offer. Whilst I was there I was offered, and accepted, a drink of Zam Zam water which I was told was very special. After we left the building Yusuf explained that Zam Zam water was from the Zam Zam well, which is inside Mecca. The water is said to have wonderful health restoring powers. I wonder how many people reading this can say they have drunk that!

That evening Yusuf said that, before he took me to the hotel I was booked into, his Mum and Dad wanted me to eat with them. He took me to his parent's home. Like most of the people I met when I was out in the direction of Erzin, his Mum was a lovely generous and kind hearted lady. They did what most Turks in that part of Turkey did, and a cloth was laid on the floor. Whilst I tried to chat with them in Turkish, bowl after bowl and plate after plate of food were brought in. Tables weren't used. I always struggled as they sit cross-legged or on their knees, and I'm not really built for that!

As we were about to sit, the doorbell rang and a couple came in, I was introduced and got the feeling that the guy was someone that Yusuf and his family respected, even looked up to. I was introduced, but at the time I couldn't for the life of me remember his or her names. I do remember though, that as the man went to sit down to eat, he lifted the flap at the rear of his jacket up so he wouldn't sit on it and I clearly saw the handle of a small pistol poking out of belt! That was a first!

During the meal the woman stayed quiet most of the time, but the man asked me a vast array of questions; where I was from, why I was in Turkey, why I was doing what I was doing, and on and on. I did my best to answer as best as I could in Turkish, with some help from Yusuf. He did at one stage look quite startled when Kismet, Ahmet and Ozzie were mentioned. I found out the reason why much later. At the end of the evening the couple got up to go and I said I'd go back to the hotel at the same time so we all went outside together. The couple climbed into a large dark coloured Mercedes, a car that may well have been thought of as old fashioned back in the UK, but in Turkey it was very much an unusual car, owned and run by people who had more money than the average Turk.

After they pulled away, I seem to remember saying something about Mafia cars, and Yusef gave me such an odd look. But he did explain that the man used to be his boss and owned, amongst other things, a bus company.

I got home the next day, armed with information regarding the licence and was ready for my next step. The website was coming along nicely, we had given the itinerary to the guy building the site, we had put descriptions of all the stopping points together, and I was in the process of putting hotel information together to add to it. Sunflower tours was ready to be born!

Again life continued, repping, guiding and generally trying to make a living. The boys were growing up quickly and had settled into school, they had large numbers of friends and were happy. Life wasn't so bad at all.

Whilst the website was being built, I received a phone call from Carole-Anne inviting me to Erzin, as she and Yusuf had decided to get engaged. I was happy for them, as they seemed made for each other. I had a few weeks to prepare myself, and decided that, since it was during the school holidays, I would take the boys with me. I had been putting lots of business to my friend with the car rental shop and it was pay-back time   He was happy to lend me a small car for a few days. I had this arrangement with him throughout my life in Turkey. If I put enough business his way, I could have a car whenever I needed one. This is how business works in Turkey to a degree. You need to go with the flow!

The boys and I set off to Erzin in good moods. However, Aslan's mood soon changed when he started to feel ill, which happened a lot on the road from Alanya to Erzin. I had to stop the car a few times so he could be physically ill, and it turned into the longest journey ever!

We arrived in Osmaniye, a town near to Erzin where there was a nice hotel. We checked in, and once Aslan felt better, we decided to go for a walk and have a look around Osmaniye, maybe grab something to eat. We left the hotel, and as it was Saturday, the place was busy outside. We walked from the hotel and I remember being dressed from head to toe in black. Black jeans and a long sleeved black top. It's important to know what I was wearing because within 100 metres of the hotel doorway, I stepped off the kerb, travelled what felt like several thousand feet before I hit the road, broke into a massive wobble on the drain I had hit, and did a triple backflip followed by a half salchow before hitting the road. This all happened in slow motion it seemed, and to add insult to injury there was something white on the road. I don't know what it was, but I know where it went! So when I eventually got to my feet, I was covered and I looked a little like the negative of a zebra! My boys were absolutely killing themselves laughing, not a move to help me up or brush my clothes down, not a move to check if I had broken anything important, just floods of laughter. I looked around me as you do after a fall, and it seemed like the whole street had stopped to look at THE foreigner playing silly buggers in the street! That moment in time will remain with me forever, and I'm hoping that one day I will see my boys, one at a time, fall down so I can 'help' them in return. For anyone who hasn't visited Turkey, there are many very high kerbs there. I've been told lots of different reasons why the kerbs are like that, ranging from they are high to stop drunk drivers running people down on the pavement, to it being a way to help control the floods. Take your pick, but I like the drunk driver explanation.

Needless to say we headed back to the hotel! I did laugh at the situation, but only when I found it funny, about 9 years later.

That evening was the engagement party and we drove to Erzin and I followed the directions I had been given, which led to a low building, a little like any social club here in the UK. I was nervous as we walked in. I knew Carole-Ann and Yusuf of course, but didn't think I'd recognise Yusuf's parents. We walked in rather sheepishly, but within a couple of minutes I was shaking hands with everyone. I vaguely remember that the man I'd met at Yusuf's home kissed me on both cheeks and then vanished. Carole-Anne appeared in a burgundy coloured meringue style dress. She was only tiny, but the dress looked enormous. I found out later that Carole-Ann had been poured into that dress, I'm assuming that Yousuf's Mum had given it to her. Carole-Ann was a size 12 and the dress was a size 8! Carole-Ann was rebelling that night, under her big dress, she had on a pair of knee high boots. She wasn't 'allowed' to drink alcohol, so Yusuf spent all night putting whiskey into her can of cola. At some point during the party, Carole-Anne's dress burst open!

I spoke to Yusuf briefly, and someone bought the boys and I something to drink. A short time afterwards, the boys and I were pulled up to dance. It was a Turkish dance where everyone held hands and danced around in a circle, I love to do this. I was aware that 'that man' was there again and I was now holding his hand, and the boys and I were whizzing around the floor like everyone else! We had a great time. When it was time to leave, we made our farewells and once again, 'the man' grabbed me, kissed both cheeks and said Good night.

Shortly afterwards, the website went live. I was away!

Shortly after this an American lady made contact with me, she worked in the US Embassy in Istanbul and had stumbled onto our website by accident when looking for a tour. We spoke a lot and she loved our tour, she thought that she could fill a minibus up regularly, in fact she was convinced she could fill it up weekly or fortnightly during the season, and in return she wanted a couple of free tours for her and her family. I was happy with this!

We had started making a few provisional dates, but nothing in concrete, for the following year. Then I got a call from her apologising and saying that she would need to cancel everything we had planned so far... why, well the Afghanistan war had started and the US soldiers weren't allowed to holiday in Turkey.

Downhill from there.... Hello and Goodbye Sunflower Tours, was nice knowing ya!

Earrings Next Time?

As I am writing this during the Covid 19 lock down, we all know how important the NHS is. Well, I realised back then how lucky we were to have a free Health service as everything needed to be paid for in Turkey. The government hospital was always so very busy and really never matched up to the standards here in the UK, and private hospitals were not the cheapest places to go.

Several times, both myself and my boys used the hospitals in Turkey. Timing was good, and I was working in some way when we needed help, so we used one of the private hospitals in Alanya.

One afternoon, I was sitting on the balcony completing some paperwork for my job with Airtours. Kaan came wandering out and sat at the table beside me. Mum? He says. Yes son, what's up, I replied rather preoccupied with my paperwork. 'If you get something stuck in your ear, what would they do'? Without even looking up I jokingly replied that the hospital would have to cut your head off, wash it out and then stitch it back on! I know, I know, but we have all said something as stupid without thinking it through. The noise Kaan made was a cross between a strangle gasp and a gurgle. I looked up to see the colour draining from his face.

'What's wrong'? I ask, my attention now fully on Kaan and his greying complexion. It all floods out, he's put a bead in his ear and can't get it out! After a few questions, it turns out that it's a little plastic beebee gun pellet! We try everything to get it out, I slosh water into his ear then turn his head so it might dislodge the bead. I daren't try with tweezers in case I push it in deeper, so the only option is to head to the local hospital.

Luckily, as we did spend a fair bit of time in there over the years, the hospital was only a ten minute walk away. We arrived and went into their version of the A & E department at the hospital, 'The Baskent'. We explained what had happened and we were taken into a small room, it was quiet as it was a Sunday. Now, bear in mind my little lad was as cute as a button, he could speak Turkish and wasn't shy! Within ten minutes Kaan had four of the prettiest nurses all buzzing around him, trying lots of simple things, pretty much like I did. That didn't work but then another very pretty nurse appeared with some long stemmed slightly bent scissor tweezers. Whilst the other nurses all continued to purr and chat to Kaan, saying how sweet and cute he was, she pulled a tiny bright blue plastic bead out of Kaan's ear! Everyone then started drifting away and Kaan came up to me, he wanted to whisper! I bent over asking what was wrong, thinking he was just a little embarrassed at all the fuss he'd been getting. 'Mum!', he whispered. 'What's up' I reply. 'Mum, I've got one in the other ear!'

All the remaining nurses, when they found out what he'd done, continued fawning over him and laughing at the situation, much to Kaan's chagrin.

The same nurse who helped retrieve the first bead, then pulled a yellow bead from Kaan's other ear! She was lovely and was so sweet to my son, she took a tiny little plastic bag from a drawer, put both beads into it and presented it to Kaan saying ' Kaan, please make a necklace next time, not earrings!'

That little trip cost me most of my wages for guiding for a week, but it was almost worth it for a funny Sunday afternoon outing, and the fact that it gave me a topic to join in with during our evening dinner conversations years later. It's always a good stand-by for when Kaan brings a girlfriend home.

But I can never say too much, in case he should ever find out that I had a similar trip to the hospital when I was small. In my case it was a bead stuck up my nose!

The 'Man'. The Mafia?

I'd spoken to a man called Olmez a couple of times when I was outside the office where the buses waited for their guides and reps. It was only a short walk from our apartment so I always walked across at the last minute. I could wait on my balcony, and when I saw my coach, Isuzu or minibus pull in, I could put my cup down and walk across to the bus. Olmez was there waiting for guides sometimes, and would always say Hello. I found him a little creepy most of the time, but I couldn't put my finger on the reason why!

One day Olmez was hanging about outside my apartment block door as I walked out. He approached me and said he wanted to talk to me. He had a message from Cevat. 'Who?' He went on to explain that Cevat was the 'man' the man I'd eaten dinner with at Yusuf's house, and the man who spoke to me at the party. I told Olmez that I didn't really know Cevat, I'd only met him very briefly. But Olmez insisted that Cevat wanted to talk to me. I'm ashamed to say I brushed him off, I didn't know Cevat and I really was very unsure of Olmez.

Over the next few weeks, this became a kind of a ritual, bumping into Olmez quite often. There was a very popular fruit and veg shop on the corner near my apartment, and he always seemed to be there. It was starting to get on my nerves, so one day I took a little more time and asked what the hell Cevat wanted, and why? Olmez said Cevat wanted to talk to me about business, he thought I could help him with something! Yeah sure, a man who lived a 14 hour drive away, sure that would help me make a living. Anyhow, Olmez said Cevat wanted to have a meeting, and that he would be in Alanya within the next few days. Could he have my phone number to pass to Cevat? I only had the mobile I'd been given by Airtours to use as I was guiding so gave him that number. We were getting towards the end of the season so I wouldn't have the phone long, so if either of them turned weird, I wouldn't care!

I was very surprised when later the same day my phone rang, and the voice on the other end was unknown. Warm, and with a nice accent, it turned out to the MAN himself. Cevat! I was surprised, little bit mixed up as to why he wanted to talk to me, and I really didn't know what to think when he started to tell me he had been trying to get my number and arrange a meet for weeks! I tried my best to speak to him in Turkish, but talking on the phone in a second language was, for me I found, difficult. But we managed between us to arrange to meet the following week. Olmez would pick me up. We arranged the time and said bye.

Much to my further amazement, each evening I got a text from Cevat, just to say he hoped I was good, and saying Goodnight! I found that really odd from the sort of man Cevat seemed to be.

The day of the meeting arrived and I had no idea where we were going, what I should be wearing, or what to expect, but I had done stranger things! Olmez arrived driving Cevat's car and Cevat was sitting in the back. I couldn't see him when I first approached the car because there were curtains up at the back and rear windows. I climbed in, rather amused, and sat next to Cevat. We drove up the mountain, stopped at a restaurant and went in. Cevat had been talking to me about general stuff, he seemed to have spent a lot of time in Alanya and seemed to know it well.

It was cold up on the side of the mountain, it must have been somewhere near the end of October, and it was about 6pm. We chose a table near an open fire, meals were ordered and the conversation continued. I swear, we talked for a couple of hours and it was really about nothing! We left the restaurant, and laughed a lot as we all had bright red tomato faces from sitting next to the hot open fire.

I was dropped off outside my apartment, Cevat got out and came round to me and said he hoped he could see me again, as we had lots to talk about! I was still lost, but said yes, he was good company.

I continued to get the texts each evening, and a few during the day. About 5 days later I 'bumped into' Cevat in the local fruit and veg shop. We laughed at the odd situation, and he asked me to walk across the road and have a coffee with him. I did, he was a nice guy, polite, and a gentleman. As we sat talking I guessed he was maybe 5 years older than me. Through previous conversations, I had learned that he owned a bus company with varying different size coaches, Isuzu's and minibuses. He had contracts in and around Erzin, and during the seasons he normally had contracts in Bodrum and Marmaris using the buses for airport transfers. He also owned lots of citrus groves, acres of them all along the coast from Antalya up to Hatay.

To cut what could be a very long story short, I was being courted, wooed, whatever you would call it, but not for marriage. Much later Cevat told me he was nervous, but so wanted to get to know me! He said that from the first meeting with me, he was impressed; with my desire to work and earn a living and at my determination. He was impressed I had learned as much Turkish as I had, he thought I was lovely! I guess that got past me, since I really wasn't used to being wooed, and I quite liked it. Now, this bit was difficult, but I knew he was married. I'd met her. He didn't talk much about her, other than to say she was miserable, they never laughed, she wouldn't travel with him or get involved in anything to do with either of his businesses, and they were really just together now as it was

131

easy! He spent at least 8 months of each year away from home and he said he had never been unfaithful to his wife, and I believed him. I knew what I was walking into.

We spent a lot of time together over the next few weeks, he bought me a phone as my Airtours phone was taken back from me, and he wanted to be able to stay in contact. He explained that he knew Yusuf, Kismet and Ahmet as they had all worked for him, he even chuckled when he told me he had sacked Kismet and Ahmet as he thought they had been stealing Diesel from him. He took me to unusual places where tourists never went to eat, soup restaurants which, if you have ever experienced them, you will know that they serve THE best food ever. He hadn't met the kids, I didn't want to introduce them to anyone until I was sure he would stick around for a while, and be good to the boys.

He even asked me, early in our relationship to go to a business meeting with him. He explained that if 'people' thought he had an English business partner that it was kudos for him. We went to the meeting and to be fair, I blagged my way through it, remained professional and as Cevat had consumed raki, I drove his car, him and a couple of the guys we had met with back down into Alanya. One of them said to Cevat as we pulled up, ' wow she's a good driver, she drives like a man!' I think was as high a compliment as you can get from a Turkish man !

Slowly, I introduced the boys to Cevat and they all got on like a house of fire. He would spoil them and would let me use his car to go collect them from school. They loved that, as the car, depending on your point of view, either looked like a politician's car or a mafia car!

If Cevat had things to do over the weekend, he would ask me to go, and would ask if the boys wanted to go too. He was a good influence, as he was firm but very fair with them and didn't' let them get away with anything that I wouldn't.

Cevat will pop up again in my stories. We were only together for just over a year, but I had some adventures as a result. We officially went into a tour business together. It was a small shopfront in Alanya from where we would sell boat trips, jeep safaris, Turkish nights etc. to tourists roaming the streets or heading back to their hotel. The season after we met, he moved his bus fleet to Alanya, which was planned to mainly do work for us. We had spent some of the winter months putting a tour of part of the silk route together. Once again I worked hard to find the route, we wanted to put guests up in Bedouin style tents, and let them travel during the day by camel! We had sourced the tents, we had found a man with camels who thought it was a great idea, we had contacted a friend of Cevat's with trucks that could move the tents and then set them back up daily, and we had spoken several times to a guy who had belly dancers, a Turkish dance troop and a couple of singers so that we could have nightly entertainment. We hadn't sorted the food yet and we hadn't sorted a website, but we had plans! But the year we planned this was 2003 and the second gulf war broke out! Once again War and Terrorism had come between me and my dreams. I gave up on opening a business then. The first gulf war almost stopped me getting Erkan's visa, the capture of the leader of the PKK Kurdish terrorists put my hotel plans out of business, the Afghanistan war was the end of Sunflower Tours and the second Gulf War put my silk road tour business out of action and almost closed my little tour shop! You couldn't' make it up!

Anyway, as I said, we visited a few places together and had a few adventures. He was, I'm pretty sure, mixed up with the Mafia, but he would rather just do an honest day's work, and he worked very hard.

Cevat told me he loved me, very early on in our relationship. We shocked people that knew him before we were 'together' and a couple of his drivers said they'd never seen him like he was when he was with me. It went wrong due to the fact that no money was coming into Turkey for tourism. I couldn't keep tripping down to Erzin with him to improve the Citrus business, and although he once took Mum, the boys and I to see a fabulous apartment in that part of the world, I wouldn't move there. It truly was an interesting chapter of my life, which I don't regret though!

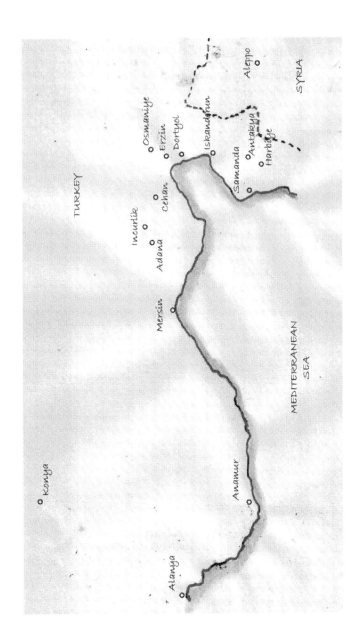

136

Indiana Jones Beat Me To This Place!

Most people will have seen Indiana Jones and the Last Crusade film, but maybe you never realised that in the film the search for the grail started in Iskenderun in Turkey. Its also known as Alexandretta. I've been lucky enough to see a lot of this part of the world, but Indy beat me to it. Cevat lived in a small town near Osmaniye which is in the Eastern side of Turkey, between Adana and Hatay also called Antakya. Hatay used to be called Antioch and was part of Syria. It was fully taken over by the Turks in 1939, and it has a wide mix of cultures and religions. This in my opinion makes it one of the most interesting places in Turkey. Istanbul is amazing, but Hatay, due to it's location and the fact that it's not rammed full of tourists, does it for me.

It was a great trading place on the silk route and St Peter built the first Christian church there. The city isn't beautiful, although the river Orontes does run through the middle, but it is just such a mix and it absolutely fascinates me. I went there many times with Cevat, but I also took the boys there for a few days. Mum and I went on a mad Christmas shopping trip once. We travelled on a coach overnight, shopped all day, as the prices and items available were far better than in Alanya, and then we travelled back overnight on the coach fully loaded with clothes for the boys, food, and Christmas presents. Mum and I freaked out on the way back, we were sitting in the front two seats on the coach, opposite from the driver. Bear in mind that this was one of the craziest roads, and very dangerous in places, AND the fact it was pitch black because it was night time. I looked up from napping to see the driver rolling a cigarette and steering with his knees! I must have made an involuntary gasp or moved oddly, and I woke my Mum who was napping as the side of me. She saw what I was looking at, and we both sat in complete silence watching. I daren't say anything for fear or making the driver jump and therefore crash! Needless to say we didn't sleep much for the rest of the journey!

The museum in Hatay has one of the best collections of Roman and Byzantine mosaics. One of my favourite things about Hatay is the numerous shops making and selling soap. Daphne, Olive oil and all kinds of wonderful smelling ingredients. I would always leave with a kilo or two or the freshly cut blocks of soap. In these times of saving the world, it is becoming fashionable again to use shampoo bars to wash hair, but all along Hatay soap has been the best thing to wash your body and hair. It was certainly good enough for Cleopatra!

Whenever we were visiting Hatay and planned to be there for a day or two, we would use hotels in Reyhanli which is a region of Hatay. There were always lots of lunch and dinner meetings, and sometimes meetings in fruit packing factories, but we did have spare time and Cevat was happy to show me some of the places that few tourists ever got to. In view of the recent war in Syria, and the large numbers of refugees going across the border, and all the problems associated with that, I doubt few tourists will ever get there again. Indeed, some of these special places are no longer there to see, it is such a sad thing.

I'd like to share a few of the places I visited. Reyhanli is a town on the outskirts of Antakya that sits on the border of Turkey and Syria. It is now war torn, just bombed buildings and lots of refugees who crossed the border out of Syria thinking they would be back in their own homes a few months later. Cevat and I drove across that border, one particular day when we had no meetings planned until an evening meal meeting. I have to say that I can't remember much fuss to drive into Syria, but we are talking about many years ago. Cevat had been across a couple of times and it was easy.

About a two hour drive later, we were in Aleppo, wandering around the streets heading for the bazaar, as they were my favourite places! The buildings were all as old as I had imagined, it was after all, one of the oldest inhabited cities in the world. The bazaar was very similar to the old bazaars in Hatay, except that it was Arabic being spoken, although some of the traders spoke a little Turkish. We wandered around and then sat down for lunch. Now, I for one don't like hot spicy food. Hatay and that region in Turkey are particularly well known for very hot spicy food! If that wasn't enough, in almost every restaurant there would be a small bowl of hot red pepper flakes (pul biber) to be scattered onto of the already spicy food! So sitting in the middle of Aleppo, I decided to wimp out and I ordered parsley soup. I know, it is wimpy, but I really didn't like to have my eyeballs and teeth melting when trying to eat! I did also have something very much like Turkish Kunefe which is a really nice cheesy, syrupy desert. Cevat went for the 'hot' food option and sprinkled red pepper on top just in case it wasn't spicy enough!

After lunch and a few glasses of tea, we headed up to the Aleppo Citadel, which is a castle high on a hill which overlooks the city of Aleppo. I'm sad now that I didn't have a camera with me, and way back then phones didn't have cameras on them. I just have my memories of wandering round the citadel in very hot weather. We left Aleppo and drove back to Reyhanli. Never would I have thought that in a few years, this amazing place would be at the centre of a devastating war. I don't know how much of Aleppo and the citadel is left, but I hope one day that tourists and adventurers get to see it.

During a trip to Samandag to check out some citrus groves that were for sale, we walked through an amazing tunnel called Vespasian's Tunnel, and we visited a massive graveyard. Wonderful sections of history.

Another time we visited Harbiye waterfall, with a collection of cafés and restaurants scattered along the riverbank.

And a special memory was our trip to The Church of St Peter in Hatay itself. It was a cave which was carved into the mountain side, and is one of Christianity's oldest churches. I took the boys to see it when we had our brief trip to Hatay, but all they saw was a cave! One day though they might appreciate that they also saw things that are amazing!

And back to where this started, Iskenderun, a big city on the coast, big harbour area and a beach. And some wonderful shopping! Again, on the occasions I visited, not a tourist in sight. I remember walking into a restaurant and the conversations all stopped. It was spooky and funny at the same time. They got over it though.

These are just a few of the fabulous places I've seen and I know how very lucky I am to have seen them, to have been there and to have such special memories.

A Fishy Tale

The boys loved to go fishing and I need to share this little gem.

One day, the boys, as was normal, collected the money they needed to buy bait, gathered up all their fishing tackle and the lunch I'd packed up. They kissed me, said Goodbye and they were off. It was a Saturday and if memory serves me well, it was out of season. They were normally up and out quite early, but it was such a performance. Their fishing tackle was stored on the balcony of their bedroom, but if they hadn't stored it properly the last time they used it, it was chaos when they came to get it out the next time. Today was no different, and we had gone through the arguments and them blaming each other, but finally they were off.

I don't know how I filled that day but I was definitely home when they appeared much later in the evening. As the apartment door opened they were chattering and extremely animated. It stopped me dead as they normally came through the door as they left, bickering and moaning at each other. But this evening, they were super pleased with themselves.

They burst into the room I was in and both of them started telling me the same story at exactly the same time. I calmed them down and they told me this story;

They had bought bait and gone to their normal fishing spot on the harbour walls, some of this wasn't real walls, just large boulders that had been placed together. The kids would all climb on these to fish from if they couldn't get on the 'proper' harbour area. But this particular day they managed to get a spot on the harbour, in spite of it being packed because there was a fishing competition taking place that day. They told me that they hadn't known about the competition in advance, but that they had simply sat and caught fish as they normally did. As the day wore on, they said that people, who I assume were the judges, started walking around counting the fish that the anglers had caught. My pair won the bloody match with the most fish in their bag. They were full of themselves, Kaan handed me a trophy he had in a plastic carrier bag, and he was so pleased with himself. I looked at the trophy and did smile. Typically Turkish, it was recycled! It was a huge trophy with three columns and a plinth. But if you looked at the plaque on the front, it was for a horse racing event some years previously. This detail didn't bother the boys at all.

To top if off, Aslan pulled 20 million Turkish Lira out of his pocket (in those days 20 million was something stupid like £10!) They had won 30 million, but had treated themselves to a kebab and cola for lunch. I was astounded, absolutely astounded!

The next day, I remember I was just taking a piece of cross stitch work into a local shop to get it framed when I was stopped by a neighbour who was just then coming out of the tobacconist shop, next door to the shop I was about to enter. He congratulated me on the boys' win. Eh? How did he know? He laughed and held up the local newspaper. There on the front page, grinning like Cheshire cats and holding a huge trophy, were my boys. After I'd left my work at the framers, I nipped in and bought a paper. There in all their glory, my boys, the writ-up explaining that two brothers had beaten seasoned anglers to the trophy in Alanya harbour the previous day.

Aslan was going through an odd stage with clothing (like Kaan's love affair with red wellies), and although he was young teenager, he insisted on wearing the same clothes as often as he could. This was a pair of well-loved jeans, I can't remember the brand name but they had a strange red eye-style logo. They were way too short but he still wore them, and he wore them with sandals and socks! And here he was in all his glory on the front page of the local paper! I cut that newspaper article out, had it framed, and it hung on my apartment wall for years.

But now, the best part. My boys are now men, both serving in the British Army. That is ironic, because they really didn't want to do National Service in Turkey, which was one of the reasons for coming back to the UK. But once back in the UK, they both joined up when they were old enough. Anyway, we were all sitting around the dinner table when they were home on leave at the same time, which unfortunately doesn't happen very often. I'm not sure how the subject came up, but they do still like to bicker and argue, and tell stories about each other at the dinner table. It is certainly an entertaining time of day when they are home together.

This particular story was however a bit of an eye opener. They slipped up badly when telling the story at dinner recently, and I learned the whole story of what had happened on that day of the Big Fishing Competition all those years ago.

They had indeed found a spot on the harbour as they had told me. But, after they had only been sitting there for about an hour, one of the men they normally sat near had come over and handed them his catch, as he had been called home. He had handed over a massive catch. They sat there the rest of the day and only caught one or two each! So the trophy, the money, the fame! The little buggers had never let on for years.

They made another slip up at a dinner conversation recently too, and it was very funny, although more difficult to describe in a way that does it justice. They were doing their usual bickering act when one of them mentioned Aslan's skipping school. Aslan had hated school, he tried very hard not to attend much of the time. Had he spent the same amount of effort inside school as he spent trying not to go to school, he would have been a rich CEO by now. There was a period when I would take him to the school gates and stand there watching him go in. What I didn't know was, that after I watched him go in, he went down into the school canteen and climbed out of a window at the back of the school, and then out of the gate where the delivery people used. I spoke to his headmaster and asked if they could call me if Aslan didn't turn up, but they were unwilling to do that, even when I volunteered to pay the bills. With 60 kids in most classes I can't blame them for not wanting to spend time on kids that didn't want to be there, but it was agony for me.

Well at this particular dinner conversation, the second funny story I want to share slipped out. Now, I didn't know that Kaan was sometimes skipping school too, but he had been involved in a couple of 'unauthorised' days out with his brother. One day they had gone up the hill towards the castle. They had been messing about on a wall, which worried me when they told me, but it did happen fifteen years ago. There had been a group of kids, including mine, and during this messing about Aslan had dropped his backpack. It was a bright blue backpack with a bright red Spiderman picture on it. Kaan made us howl when he did a pantomime of Aslan trying to reach his backpack, but it had fallen into the sea and started drifting off towards Cyprus. Kaan had explained that Aslan was frantic but could do nothing. Now this is the part that is hard to do justice to, but it really tops the story off. Imagine how you walk if you had a back pack on and you had hooked your thumbs through the straps at the front. Aslan had been practising this all the way home with an imaginary backpack. When he got through the apartment door, my Mum was in the kitchen. He confidently walked past the kitchen door with his thumbs tucked in his invisible backpack with a cheeky 'Hi Nan' and Mum never noticed his backpack was missing. They had other backpacks so I had never found out Spiderman had gone swimming.

As much as Aslan was a devil skipping school, Kaan was a devil on a little yellow bike he had. We had taken it out from the UK with us, as it was to be his Christmas present. He used it until he was far too big for it, and then he finally allowed us to replace it for him, but even then he was not really very willing. He was a little speedy on that bike, and every time I knew he was going out on it, we would have the same conversation, about him not going far on it, staying near the apartment, not going over the roads without hitting the button and walking across, particularly the very busy roads. He said all the right things in reply. But, on one particular day I was sitting in my rented Red Fiesta, about to head off to Belek for my transfer job. Way back then, driving in Turkey was only for the brave. If you pulled up at traffic lights and it was meant for there to be two lanes of traffic, you would normally see four and sometimes five lanes form, ready to race away when the lights changed, or more usually just before the lights changed. Well, this day I was sitting at a set of lights not far from home, on one of the three main roads that run through Alanya. The lights changed but no one could move. Everyone was beeping at a little boy on a bright yellow bike, going as fast as he could alongside another boy. They were laughing their little heads off as they crossed the road holding all the traffic up. Yes one of them was indeed Kaan! We had words the following day!

In their defence though, they have grown into truly wonderful young men. Both serving in the British Army, both have started climbing the ranks and continue to do so. Both are smart, good looking boys but not arrogant or self-centred in any way. Whatever I did or didn't do when living out there. I did well with the boys. I'm an extremely proud Mum.

Lunch with the Mafia

Cevat and I were down in Iskenderun and we got into the car one morning when his phone rang. He answered and then spoke quite sharply to whoever was on the other end. He looked angry when he turned to tell me that the meeting we were due to attend, which was about supplying citrus fruit to Odessa in the Ukraine would have to be rearranged as he had been called to a meeting in Ceyhan which was a couple of hours drive away. Cevat made a couple of calls, one to cancel our meeting and then he stepped out of the car, and made another. He wandering backwards and forwards along the side of the car and I could see and hear that he was incredibly angry about something.

He took his jacket off and got back into the car, there was little point asking if he was Ok, as he would never tell me of any problems, he was very old fashioned in some ways and some things were just not told to women! But I trusted him, indeed I trusted him with my life, as we had travelled to places that were truly 'out of bounds' to some people and particularly to an English woman!

I settled down for the journey and Cevat relaxed a little. On the journey to Ceyhan, we stopped after about 90 minutes at a little place. It was almost a shed, but turned out to belong to a lovely little man and his wife who had set up their little business on the side of the road. It was in a wooded area on a windy road and their 'shed' was set in one of the curves and had enough empty land in front of it to pull the car on. We sat outside at a tiny little wonky table on two old mismatched chairs. The old lady, who was hunched over as she walked, served us both tea and asked if we wanted something to eat. Cevat asked for Pestil, something I'd never heard of before, and the old lady scuttled off. She returned soon after and offered us the Pestil that Cevat

147

had ordered. It was the oddest thing I'd ever seen, and although I tried a little, it wasn't really something I could eat, even to be polite. Cevat on the other hand chewed it whilst drinking his cups of tea, and asked that the lady wrap it up so he could take what was left away with us. The nearest translation for this food was 'Fruit leather', and it was like sucking a piece of old satchel to me!

We were off again and Cevat's mood had lightened, he explained that he had been called to a meeting, and he really didn't want me to be anywhere near it, but asked if I would wait in the car. I'd done that before, this country was, and probably always will remain a man's world and even though I didn't agree with that, or like it, I wasn't in a position to change it, and sometimes women were just not accepted. I was fine with waiting in the car, and it turned out that was the place to watch everything unfold!

We got to Ceyhan and it took Cevat a little time to find where the meeting was to take place, we found the restaurant, which was quite odd, not a shed, but a long building, almost like the old portacabins that schools in the UK brought in when the pupils started bulging out. So imagine two, possible three portacabins side my side, lengthways, the side facing us had low windows, and it was raised up on stilt like supports. There were a set of steps in the middle leading up to the building itself, with the name of the restaurant on a sign which ran along the top of the building.

We must have been the first to arrive as there were no other cars in the huge car park in front of the building. As we parked up, I could feel that Cevat was tense, which was unusual. I'd known him almost a year and had never seen him nervous, scared or bothered about anything or anyone before, he seemed to be made of steel!

He got out of the car and put his jacket on, he was a typical Turkish 'business man' and his suit was quite old fashioned, a pin striped jacket and trousers, but he was smart. He then did something that put me on edge, he reached under his seat and pulled out the cloth bag that hid his Baretta pistol!

Now how, you're thinking, do I know what that was? Well a few months earlier, Cevat and I had been travelling back from Hatay. The roads, for anyone who has been lucky enough to travel along the road from Alanya to Hatay will tell you, are exciting, nerve racking and for passengers, sick making! The road follows the contours of the coast line but as well as just being twisty and turny, some parts of the road having nothing at the side to stop you crashing down the side of the mountain, some parts in the winter having a massive amount of water running down the mountain side and gushing down and across the road. It was also up and down like being on a roller coaster. If you were driving and concentrating, it wasn't so bad, but as a passenger... it was sick making! It was many hours to get from Hatay to Alanya, and due to the poor road and the geography of this part of the Mediterrean was, and still is, the least spoilt and under developed. If you ever get the opportunity, then go see what I am talking about!

Anyhow, again I digress. This particular road was, however, a busy route for smugglers, especially during the night, which is when Cevat and I normally travelled it. From previous stories you will know I'd glimpsed Cevat carrying a gun, but never close up! Because the road was being used to smuggle, anything from cigarettes and alcohol to antiquities and weapons, it was patrolled by the Turkish Gendarma. This is a service branch of the Turkish Ministry of Interior, responsible for the maintenance of public order in areas that fall outside the jurisdiction of police forces. In other words, they were armed soldiers and a lot scarier than the normal Turkish police who could be scary enough! Occasionally, they would create a roadblock along this deserted stretch of road, normally just round a bend so they were out of sight until it was too late to do anything other than stop politely!

On this particular journey, Cevat and I stopped at a Gendarma road block, middle of the night, coming to face with 5 or 6 armed soldiers is a little daunting, trust me on that one, and as we pulled up Cevat pulled his pistol out of his waistband and handed it to me! I was instructed to put it in my handbag and speak lots of English. Cevat knew very little English but I did as I was asked, I slipped the small, warm pistol into my handbag that I kept on the floor next to my feet. As the windows were wound down the Gendarma started looking in the car. The back and rear windows had curtains up, obstructing their view, so they opened the back doors and the boot, whilst they started asking Cevat questions. Not quite sure what I should do and who I should talk to in English, I decided to talk to myself. I took my phone out of my bag, held it up to my ear and started prattling away in English, telling myself we had been stopped by the Gendarma blah de blah! The Gendarma looked at me but did no more, and a few minutes later they waved us on! Cevat was laughing and said thanks as I handed the pistol back to him! Apparently, he told me, I had less chance of being searched as I was speaking English, very few of the Gendarma spoke a second language and would be 'put off' by me   He told me his gun was a Baretta and he carried it because he, as I knew well by then, carried a lot of cash with him sometimes, and wasn't prepared to be a sitting target!

So back to the restaurant. Cevat pulled the pistol from the bag it was kept in and tucked it down the waistband in the small of his back. He leant into the car and told me not to worry and closed the door and headed in! I sat there, trying hard not to worry But the next 30 minutes really didn't help with that. Car after car pulled up alongside Cevat's. All very similar cars, all Mercedes, all black, or occasionally dark blue, Mercedes S500. Big, sturdy, powerful cars. Remember this was a long time ago, before Turkey became as prosperous and popular, before the ladies with headscarves all started driving around in brand new small cars! These were the days when the Turks would keep their cars and vans on the road by whatever means possible.

Most of the cars had two men in them, and as they climbed out of their cars, all dressed in the same style as Cevat, all a similar age, they each would automatically check under their jackets to the small of their backs, and it was evident to me that they were all carrying hand guns! Continuing to 'try not to worry' was not so easy! All the men walked up the steps and into the building, all had to walk past the car I was sitting in, so I had a front row seat to whatever was about to take place.

The next surprising thing was when a waiter came out of the restaurant with a tray in his hand. He walked up to the car and knocked on the window. Cevat had sent lunch out for me! I opened the door, a tray containing a cold drink and a selection of small starters and bread was handed to me, and the door was closed.

For the next hour, I sat picking at the food and sipping the drink, watching the scene in front of me. It seemed that the men had divided into clear groups inside the restaurant. None of them were eating, but all of them had glasses of raki in their hands. After a few minutes it became very clear that they were starting to argue. I hadn't seen Cevat for a few minutes, then he came nearer to the window, and I could see how incredibly angry he looked! I can honestly say it was like watching a bad movie, and I was truly waiting for shots to be fired!

Much to my relief, about 90 minutes after Cevat and I had pulled up outside, the first of the men started to leave the restaurant. All were angry, some throwing things, raki glasses, tea glasses, looking totally pissed off. I had always joked to a dear friend of mine that I suspected Cevat to be in the Mafia, and that day my suspicions were confirmed. When Cevat appeared, he asked me to drive, so I climbed out of the car, put my lunch tray on the steps of the restaurant, and walked round to the driver's side and slid in. I pulled out of the car park and could clearly feel the tension within Cevat ease. He told me where to head and I drove for about 15 minutes. Not a word was spoken, it was clearly not the time for one of my flippant remarks, bad jokes, and definitely not any questions!

After this time, Cevat asked me to stop when I could, so I pulled into the next empty piece of land I saw. Cevat got out of the car and lit a cigarette. I turned the engine off and joined him. He then started to tell me I had just witnessed a meeting with the Ankara, Adana, Hatay, Mersin and the Karaman Maras mafia! He never told me why they had met, but he never told me why he was involved, and I knew better than to push any further.

Several weeks later, Cevat and I were in Erzin, and went to a late meeting. As always there were maybe two dozen men there, they were always shocked to see me with Cevat which I found quite funny, but Cevat and I were in both a business relationship and a personal relationship. The business was both generating work for the buses in his bus company, and selling and exporting the citrus fruit he was growing on the southern coast of Turkey. This meeting was about his citrus fruits and it seemed that someone had moved some fences and were trying very hard to use some of Cevat's land as their own. The meeting started very calmly, we all had a meal and the other guys were really friendly, asking me how I arrived in Turkey and that they never saw English women in that part of the world. I knew from experience that a lot of people in that part of the world had never seen a foreigner, never mind a female foreigner! I do remember the 'odd' looks I would get when Cevat took me into the typically Turkish restaurants we used to frequent. Shock, surprise, horror and even disgust sometimes. Hey ho…. Never bothered me.

During the evening the conversations got heated. I couldn't understand everything that was happening, although I could clearly get the gist! We left the meeting and Cevat asked me to drive once more, as he regularly did, but as we were driving down the quiet roads he took his bloody gun out and shot two shots out of the window up in the air! Needless to say I almost drove off the road. I lost the plot with Cevat, and he saw for the first time my English temper. He promised never to get his gun out, keep it in his waistband, or even mention it again, and he never did!

See… my life has been amazing, I have seen things, been places and done things that few women would have seen, done or been! And the story continues……..

The Billionaire in a Baseball Cap

At one point during my life in Turkey, I had made friends with a pair of brothers who were Estate Agents. I had never got involved with the Estate agency side of things in Turkey. I truly thought they were pirates, selling property at inflated prices, giving people promises that they either had no intention of keeping, or were totally unable to keep. I had sometimes helped them out with translating something simple. On one occasion, and against my better judgement, I went to view a villa with them. But I stayed in the background and just helped out with translating the odd question. I told them I didn't want to do it again. It didn't sit right with me.

Anyhow, one of the brothers contacted me one afternoon to ask for help. They had a very important potential customer who was coming to view the same villa. He was from Iraq. Their English wasn't brilliant, and although they spoke a little bit of lots of other languages, Iraqi wasn't one of them. They didn't know how good the potential client's English was, but he only spoke English and his native language.

They offered me 50 euros to help them, and if a sale was made I would get a small percentage. I had nothing planned for a couple of days so I reluctantly agreed. On the morning we agreed, I was in their office early and they seemed very nervous. When I asked why, they told me that this guy was very important and they really wanted to sell him something.

A large black 4 x 4 pulled up outside the shop and everyone jumped up. 4 men climbed out of the car, two men from the back seat, very smartly dressed in suits and shiny shoes, the driver, who was in very similar clothing. The front passenger was wearing jeans, a smart shirt and had a baseball cap on. My friends the estate agents seemed to hesitate but then decided that the guys from the back seat seemed more likely to be the boss, so they headed in their direction.

I had stayed back, I really didn't want to be there anyway, but 50 euros was 50 euros in those days. I was drawn to the guy with the baseball cap on. It just didn't seem that one man, even if he was a bodyguard or spare driver, would turn up in jeans unless he was extremely confident. He walked into the office whilst everyone else was out on the pavement. We shook hands, I introduced myself and he smiled and introduced himself. He was, of course, the potential customer.

After the embarrassing start, and once everyone was sorted out, introduced and knew who was who, coffee was offered. But it was declined, and so we headed up to the first villa in a convoy of cars. The villa was amazing, it was the one I had looked at a few weeks earlier. As we walked around and everything was explained, the luxury of it was incredible. There were even small living quarters that had been hidden in the villa's grounds. We were at the villa for quite some time, and I got a little chance to chat with Amir, as I'd discovered he was called. His English was better than mine! When I asked, he explained that he was born in Iraq but had moved with his family to the United States when he was small. He then moved back to Iraq when the war was coming to an end, as he saw an opportunity to make money with a building company.

After viewing that villa we moved on to another property, then stopped for a light lunch. Then one more villa before heading back into Alanya. I thought my time was done, but after the estate agents asked Amir to join them for dinner, he said yes and asked me to join them too.

We dined in a very nice fish restaurant and I was seated next to Amir. Property was obviously discussed by everyone, as was the state of the world. Conversations then drifted off, and it was quite normal to chat with the person seated next to you. Amir asked me about Alanya, about the surrounding cities and he congratulated me at my local knowledge. He was a nice guy, told me about his business, he had formed a building company that had prospered. He explained he had moved back to Iraq, at a huge risk, but he knew that the country would need rebuilding. He seemed to have his fingers in lots of pies and was seriously considering buying a place in Turkey so that he could escape the compound he lived in in Iraq every now and again, without travelling too far.

I ended up spending the next day looking at property, further out of Alanya, and the day played out pretty much the same as the first day. Dinner again followed, but this time we went to what I would call a typical Turkish Nightclub with live singing as entertainment. It was harder to have a conversation this time, but at one point Amir came straight out and asked me if I thought that the price for the first Villa he had been shown, which was by far the best, was a fair one. I knew that the estate agents had told him a price far higher than the first guy they showed the villa too a few weeks earlier. I knew that if Amir bought it, I would get a good commission, but I probably wouldn't have slept again. No matter if he had the cash to buy it, my thoughts were sell it at the original asking price and sell it rather than pump the price up and let it sit unwanted and unloved. So I told him. I told him it was a great villa but at that price he could get more. I advised him to put in a lower offer, and certainly not to pay anywhere near the price they were asking. He smiled and asked if I was getting commission and I said yes I was. His response was 'Thank you Tina for being honest even if it costs you money. I don't meet many people like you'. He asked for my phone number and email address.

Amir didn't buy the villa, he didn't buy any of the properties he'd been shown and he left Alanya the following day.

I carried on with my life and never imagined for one second that I would ever speak to Amir again. But I was surprised when my phone rang and the number showing started with 0964 wherever that was. But I answered anyway, and the warm well spoken English voice was familiar. 'Tina?' It was Amir. I laughed and asked him what he was up to? It turned out he wasn't 'up to anything' he just wanted to talk to someone normal, someone who didn't want anything from him, and someone with a friendly voice!

Over the next few years, Amir called me randomly to do this. I didn't know what to think. But he was always nice to talk to, but sometimes we were on the phone for an hour or more. I learnt from Amir, that his building company was an incredible success. He had started with very little but due to all the building and rebuilding work necessary in Iraq, it had boomed. He was involved with other things as well now, and this is the list I gleaned from him over the years that we spoke. He was building a 5 star hotel, he owned a bank (yes, owned), he was helping to build a new airport, he opened a business selling hardcore, aggregates and building supplies. He helped Iraq to switch to LPG gas, he had contracts for buses for school runs and oh, many others. He was a bloody billionaire!

The fact that he was calling me so that he could talk to a normal person always took me by surprise He always used a different phone number, whether he rang me twice in the same month or twice in a year. He said it was necessary as women would, by whatever means find his number, call him up and pretend to have called him by mistake. Then they would invariably become sexy and flirty, and Amir just knew that they knew who he was, and what he owned. He told me that sometimes he would egg them on for a bit of sexual chatting, but whether he did or didn't he would always start using a different phone number!

He told me lots of things. He said he had given his brother and mother a lot of money, and he was trying to hand off some of the responsibilities. I laughed many times. Could being a billionaire really be that difficult? But it seemed so. He once skyped me, and we were talking about cars. He was explaining that when he went to stay in Dubai to get away from the 'troubles' in Iraq, he was normally given a sports car to use to get about. On his last trip he been given a bright yellow Lamborghini, but he laughed as he had struggled to get into it. He was a tall man and wasn't exactly skinny. What a bummer that must have been though, hey?

He once showed me the view out of his suite window from some super luxurious hotel he was staying in for a few weeks. It was an amazing view but he wasn't happy. He was lonely, didn't trust many people, was tired of everyone always wanting something and he was just plain tired. He once said he would give everything away and take a job on a building site. I doubt he ever would, but how sad!

During one conversation about cars, he filmed himself walking out of his villa and into his garage, which was more like an underground car park than a garage. There he tormented me by showing me some of his cars. It was like a prestige showroom, with cars of varying degrees of luxury. Some were staff cars, some were his family's and some his. He wasn't showing off though, he offered me any that I wanted if I would go work for him!

Amir offered me many jobs, during the time I knew him. The first was in the hotel he was building. The second in the airport he was helping to operate. Another was something to do with the aggregates company. Even when I got back to the UK he continued to call me. When he found out I was working for a Recovery Company, he offered to start a Recovery company and let me run it. He told me that his trucks from the building company regularly travelled from Erbil into Turkey, and they regularly came across broken down vehicles, so there was enough potential work to start a business. He picked my brains and said he would buy service vans and heavy recovery vehicles, he would find translators or dual speaking staff. He even gave me the opportunity to ask any of the staff I was working with if they wanted to work out there!

As I said, he offered me many jobs. If I would move to Iraq, he said I could have a house on the same compound as him. He would find the boys a private school if I wanted to take them, or he would make sure I could fly backwards and forwards to see them as often as I wanted.

His last job offer was organising and monitoring the buses that did the school runs, a million dollar a year contract! He thought he might have to give it up as he was too busy with the gas contract!

I turned him down every time. Sometimes I was indeed almost convinced enough to find out more, but my boys, my Mum, my husband. The timing was never good. And the reason he continually asked me? Well, he told me a thousand times. He knew that I was hard-working, but more than anything else, he knew I was honest. His conversations will always stay with me, him telling me that I was worth more than I was doing, telling me how he thought about me. Coming from a man like Amir, that was worth a lot.

Our conversations drifted off until sadly they stopped, and I do hope that it's because he found a soul mate, someone who would make him happy, and most of all someone honest.

A Man's World

Now this isn't what you might think, but I would like to explain that being a lone woman in any country can be difficult. I know some women will mock me saying this is rubbish, but even in the UK, as a woman, if you approach a garage for car repairs as a lone female your bill will probably be more than a man. The same thing with quotes for building work, decorating, electricians, handymen, whatever the 'thing' I do believe that women are dealt with differently. You may disagree, but this is my personal feeling.

Now I'm not a 'burn the bra' sort of woman, but neither am I a flowery girly girl, especially after going through all I have. But I know that Turkey is, in every sense, a man's world. Being a single, foreign, woman in Turkey is NOT easy. Please don't mock me, don't say it's not true. Not unless you have lived there and experienced it yourself!

I did a lot when I lived in Turkey, I did a lot more than I should. I lived in fear sometimes, I lived with no money sometimes, but in order to get some things done, sometimes you have to eat crap, but at other times you draw the line.

Once Erkan had left, I had little time to dwell on a divorce, neither did I have the knowledge of how to go about getting things in motion. I didn't even have the cash to do it. But as time went by, I felt I was regaining control over my life, and the boys and I were doing OK. Life had certainly been worse.

I had been making reasonably good money as a rep and a guide. I'd kept going for a while with the little shop I had, but that was now closed. I had stopped going to the craft fayre other than to call in to say Hello to my friends there. I had made money with the handbag trip to Istanbul, and I had now met Cevat and plans were afoot to open a street-side tour business.

I was ready once again to take control of my life and I decided it was time to seek a divorce. It was about 15 months since Erkan had finally gone. I didn't see him. He did sometimes ring me during the night, mainly to try to mess with my mind, threatening to take the boys away and vanish with them. That frightened me to death, without Erkan travelling with us, or without something from him to say it was OK, I knew I would never get the boys out of Turkey through a Turkish airport. They, like me, had Turkish nationality and we had chosen to live here. That meant there were rules to follow.

However, I had checked up and found out that I could, if in jeopardy, get on a ferry in Alanya using our Turkish passports, get off the ferry in Turkish Cyprus, then use our British passports to travel across the border into Greek Cyprus. Once there we could use our British Passports to fly back to the UK. Complicated, but I was totally able to do this if I had needed to. I could do anything to keep my boys safe and with me.

I made enquiries and several people gave me the name of an English speaking solicitor. I could by then speak a fair amount of Turkish, but I had learned this through the need to work, so if I was doing transfers I would learn how to say, left, right, please turn the air conditioning on. When I worked in the restaurant, I learned the words for cutlery, crockery, table, chairs etc. I did however, understand considerably more than I could speak. Yet, speaking to a solicitor was a little beyond me, or so I thought.

I made an appointment and arrived at the solicitor's office on the due day at the right time. I was incredibly nervous, I was sad, but I needed to make everything official so I could sleep at night and stop worrying that my kids would vanish!

I was already aware of the Hague convention which seeks to protect children from abduction and retention across international boundaries. But Turkey is an enormous country, the Hague convention would only help if I knew where the boys were.

I had also learned through research that, in Turkey, boys over 7 were normally placed in the custody of the father. Custody for the mother was hard to gain. This made me realise why the divorce rate was so low, women don't want to leave their sons. Clearly girls weren't thought of as important!

When asked, I stepped into the solicitor's office. He was a smart guy, wearing a shirt and tie. He shook my hand and spoke to me in English. I explained everything to the solicitor, how we had originally moved here to rent and run a hotel, the breakdown in the marriage, and also that I had the doctor's and police reports, issued at the time, to support my claim of abuse. He appeared to be listening intently and asked occasional questions. He told me about the eldest son probably going to his father, but I said nothing. That would never happen. He asked for Erkan's full name and any address I had, which I couldn't help with, and he asked for Erkan's telephone number which I supplied.

He asked me to excuse him for a couple of minutes while he called Erkan. I sat there whilst he dialled. When Erkan answered, he started a conversation in Turkish with my soon to be ex-husband. The conversation lasted a few minutes. Bear in mind I could speak a fair bit of Turkish but that I could understand an awful lot more. This is how their conversation went:

Solicitor introduces himself and explains that he has Erkan's wife sitting in front of him wishing to start divorce proceedings.

Listens to what I can only imagine Erkan's reply is

Solicitor explains to Erkan that for a certain amount of money, he, the solicitor, would ensure that the soon to be ex-wife will get nothing (he clearly didn't know there was nothing to get) then he continued on to say that we would also guarantee that both boys went to Erkan!

I sat listening to the remainder of the conversation, but I had already heard enough. At the end of the conversation, the phone was put down, and the two faced, poxy, sneaky rattlesnake of a man smiled at me and said he was sure he could work for me.

I can't put into words what expletives burst forth, every swear word I had ever heard in Turkish, every expletive I had ever learned full stop. We all learn swear words first don't we? I ran out of Turkish and continued in English, and boy I know lots of English expletives. He went incredibly red. At one point I did think that his head might explode. He muttered and stumbled over words and was walking towards me. I think my words were then something like 'Save your life and stop there!'. I was, to say the least, MAD!

Needless to say, I left his office. I did want to complaint to someone about him, but never really found out who policed these guys.

A month or so later, Cevat had spoken to various people and told me he had found a good solicitor who spoke English and would sort things out properly for me. When I went to that office, Cevat had sent two of his drivers with me, they waited in the waiting room for me, but their presence was somehow comforting. The solicitor did arrange my divorce. It cost me about twice the average amount divorces were costing Turkish people, though. But that was the least of my problems.

Erkan continued to mess with my mind, right up to the night before the case was going to court. He told me that if he turned up the following day at court and said that he didn't want a divorce, that I wouldn't get one. I didn't sleep that night, as I knew that it was probably true.

The following day, my wonderful Dad came with me to the courts. We were shown into a small room when the time came, and a man in a wonderful 'Harry Potter' style outfit with gold epaulettes entered through a different door. He sat behind a desk and opened a folder in front of him. As he was reading it, he occasionally glanced up at me. He spoke to the solicitor in Turkish and I know he said 'where did she find this one?' And he signed off my divorce.

I was given full custody of both boys, and all the paperwork to confirm this, and confirm that I could leave the country with them without Erkan's consent.

Another mission accomplished!

A little note about when we were traveling in and out of Turkey. I apologise to anyone who was behind us in airport queues, as it was very time consuming. Leaving Turkey had to be on Turkish passports with the court papers, but we then had to show the British passports because we didn't have leaving permits in our Turkish passports. But we couldn't just leave on the British Passports because we didn't have Turkish entry visas. Still with me here? When Mum was traveling with the boys on her own, the above still applied for the boys, but I had to have a legal paper written for Mum to show, saying that I'd given her permission. Sorry if you were behind us!

Are You In A Safe Place?

21st March 2003. Can you remember where you were? What you were doing? I can. Cevat and I had been talking with people about the contract to bus personnel into the Oil refinery near Ceyhan. It was a massive site, with people living on it, shops, cafes, restaurants and it's own independent community, but a lot of local staff also needed to be ferried in and out daily to complete the number of workforce required. The contract was due for renewal, it was local to Cevat and his bus company, and Americans were involved. With my help, Cevat's company planned to put in a bid for it.

We travelled to the Refinery for a dinner meeting. It took forever to get through security onto the refinery site. We were shown to a big restaurant, and introduced to both the Turkish team and the Americans. The American's were surprised to be introduced to me, they said they had been expecting a Turk with good English. The meeting went well from my point of view, Cevat had told me everything I needed to know regarding the buses, and he would be speaking to the Turks regarding the price and the anticipated bids he should put forward.

The meeting then drifted to a close and we continued with our meal and an over dinner chat. It was about this time that my phone started beeping, chiming and basically going bonkers. I excused myself and left the table to check what was happening. The boys were my first thought, they were with my Mum and Dad but I always worried. I checked my texts and they were from several different friends, all asking the same seemingly random question.... 'Tina, where are you? Are you safe?' Odd question! I attempted to listen to the first of three voicemails, but before I could, my phone rang. I answered and it was a friend in Alanya asking me where I was, and was I OK? I was, I told her, what's wrong?

My friend continued to explain that America had invaded Iraq! She was worried where I was, as she knew I wasn't home! When I answered, I was sitting in a restaurant on the middle of an oil refinery! She responded with PFFFF!

Now just to explain…. the American armed forces were using Incirlik air base in Turkey to land thousands of their troops, as Turkey is a NATO country. Incirlik was not far from where we were sitting having dinner! Not many places are worth bombing in Turkey, but certainly the base where American's were flooding into the country, and oil and petrol refinery's might well have been marked with crosses on a map somewhere!

I turned my phone off. I did reply to everyone the following day to tell them I was safe though. We drove off the refinery site, Cevat was feeling optimistic about the bid he would put in for the personnel bus service, and I was feeling optimistic about getting back to Alanya the following day. Certainly nothing to bomb there.

The following day we set off in the car to Alanya. We got to one particular give way junction and stopped. We had no choice really, as there was a convoy of hundreds of American's driving past!

I was happy to get home!

Ding Ding!

I am bearing my soul with these stories, but for people who know me now, I do believe, or hope that you will not recognise the 'lady' (me) in these following anecdotes! I am mellow now, calm and patient. Don't mistake that as being a push over, I'm certainly not, but I deal with things without anger nowadays.

I had, throughout my life, always been the joker, the clown. First the girl, then the lady, with the sarcastic comment or quick funny reply. But during my 10 year stay in Turkey, I changed. Turkey is a harder place to live, the boys needed to learn how to defend themselves, and arguments tend to be settled with physical events.

Following my divorce, I became very angry. Angry at everyone, everything. I think Mum and Dad, who had by then moved out to Turkey, well, they knew me better than anyone. Fortunately they trusted me, they knew I needed to get through all this crap that was happening in my life, and they supported me and had the boys a lot of the time. They took the boys on little holidays, and made up for the absence of a father and having a mother who was having a melt down.

I had a good friend, Jules, who had moved to Turkey for her own reasons, and she was very much in the same frame of mind.

We spent almost one entire season going out every night the year following my divorce. We drank, we laughed and we wanted nothing more than our own company. At this time I was working in my own tour business out of a shop, and I was never late! To this day, I'm not sure how I did it.

171

Jules and I had a routine, which involved spending as little as possible and laughing as much as we could. But I'm ashamed to say, we had regular fights with women and men who pissed us off! As we arrived in town, normally in Jules' super little car, we would walk over to a little shop near our normal parking spot and each buy a small bottle of Turkish Vodka. This would then be transferred into water bottles, we had fortuitously taken with us! Our thinking, you see, was that in all holiday resorts, everyone carried a small water bottle around with them! Our plan worked and we were able to buy just cola in almost every club or pub we went into, and secretively pour our vodka into the cola. We were only ever questioned once by a waiter who served us nearly every night. He said he knew what we were doing and that it wasn't water in the bottles! We both took Umbridge, defending ourselves with innocent faces. Jules took it one step further and opened her bottle, she lugged it down and without a blink of an eye, then closed the top and put the bottle down. 'Could I really do that if it wasn't water?' He apologised rather sheepishly and walked away. Jules' face was a picture, and thankfully I never had to do the same thing.

We just wanted to be left alone when we went out, but there was always some twig-like foreigners who thought that two 'older women' sitting drinking and laughing were a great source of fun. One of us being fat, and the other being a bottle blonde.

One evening we were in the Robin Hood bar which was always our last stop. There were several bars on the ground floor, more bars on the second floor and on the top floor there was a Tequila Bar. We always stayed on the ground floor. We would sit at the bar, drink, laugh and sometimes dance. There was a girl serving behind one of the bars and we got to know her well, and the other bar staff all knew us.

We also knew many of the numerous bouncers dotted about in the bars and on the doors. I think they knew we were just entertaining ourselves and never meant or caused any trouble!

One evening, we were sitting at the bar laughing over something which was probably not funny to anyone else, and all the funnier since it was fuelled by Vodka. Jules pointed out a couple of girls and a Turkish guy who were behind me at the bar, and who seemed to be poking fun at us. This progressed through the evening and was really starting to get on our nerves. Why us, we weren't bothering anyone? It was the Turk who seemed to be making fun of us, and the two twigs were laughing. We thought they might be German, and they clearly had a death wish!

At one point Jules said she was off to the toilet which was on the second floor and reached by a staircase situated behind Tweedle Dum, Tweedle Dee and Dopey the Turkish comedian. As Jules walked past with her back to them they were laughing and mocking her. I could see this quite clearly, and suddenly there was a loud noise. Oh it was me snapping! And there is nothing worse than an annoyed fat woman, who is already in an angry frame of mind with everything and everybody!

What happened next is a true story, nothing added, nothing omitted. I got off my bar stool and slowly walked towards the morons who thought it was OK to try and spoil someone's night out. They didn't know either of us. We had never met before and we had never really given them any attention. As I got close they stopped talking and looked at me, smirking. Without a word, and without any warning, I slapped the Turk across the face, he left his stool sideways and did that funny walking running step thing that people do who are about to fall down and are trying to keep their balance.

173

My attention then turned to the twigs, and I think I said something like 'let's go and see what's so funny outside shall we ladies?' The smirks had left their faces now, and had been replaced by looks of fear. By now Dopey had lost his balance as well as the battle and was on the floor, he was smarter than I first thought though, as he stayed there and never tried to help his 'friends'.

I grabbed one of these piss takers by the collar and the other I had by the neck! Yes I did, for anyone who knows me now. How could I possible have done that? Well, I did. I started dragging them towards the door just as Jules reappeared at the bottom of the stairs. She laughed and asked what I was doing, and did I need a hand. I shouted back that I was sick and tired of morons who thought it was perfectly alright to take the mickey out of people minding their own business, and thanks but no, I was fine!

We got to the door and one of the bouncers approached me, asking what I was doing? I replied that I wasn't quite sure but that I'd figure something out once we got outside! He then took my new friends off me! I was a bit put out, but he made them leave the pub and we saw the Turk who had been with them sheepishly follow them out.

We went back to our drinks, Jules lit a cigarette and we started laughing. We laughed for a long time at the situation that might have developed if I had gotten through the door. Jules asked me what I would have done if I had got outside with them on my own. I would have figured something out!

We finished that night in a good frame of mind, knowing that the trio might think twice before making fun of people that were minding their own business. We had done a good deed! Hadn't we?

On another night we had wandered into a nightclub which we visited occasionally. In this club it was a bit of a pain to get to the bathrooms. The club was also almost all outside. As you walked through the gateway, you entered the seating area with tables and chairs and table service just to get a drink. There was a pathway through the middle, which headed to a dancefloor which was incredibly full most of the time during the summer months. The annoying thing was, that to reach the bathroom you had to negotiate your way across this dancefloor.

On this occasion Jules was in front and I was following in her footsteps through the throng of dancers as they kindly moved to let us though. She stopped, so I stopped. There were a group of about 6 girls, all in their 20's, and Jules was struggling to get past them. I heard Jules shout, in a friendly tone 'sorry ladies can we get past?' There was no response, she shouted again 'Come on girls let us through'. Nothing, no response and I braced myself as Jules moved forward anyway which meant that she was applying a full body tackle to two of the girls in an attempt to get through them.

One of the girls, but not one who was involved in the Rugby tackle, then opened her mouth and uttered words which I would imagine that she regretted later. She said 'What's your problem Grandma?' Whooooa! Before the girl had chance to smile at her 'funny' remark, Jules had raised her right arm and landed an open palm slap onto the chubby little cheeks of funny girl! The girl went over as she was clearly not expecting Grandma to reply, and certainly not to reply in such a spectacular way! She was lucky though, as I'd seen the results of Jules' punches. She got away with her insult quite lightly. Jules stepped over her and I followed, laughing once again at the foolish people who thought insults, being rude and generally being plebs was OK and accepted by everyone. I guess many people would have just shuffled off after the insult and then

175

spent a long time regretting not responding even verbally! Not us, not that day!

We left the bathroom and walked back over the dancefloor, but this time with no group of girls playing silly buggers! We found a table, sat down and ordered our colas! We then saw the same group of girls sitting near the dancefloor. Jules had her back towards the dancefloor when I spotted them, and I told Jules where they were. She asked me to just keep my eye on them and let her know if any or all of them approached us. We stayed for about an hour, and I gave commentary to Jules. All I could see were the girls clearly trying to encourage each other to come and 'speak' to Jules! But none of them seemed inclined to! The girl with the smart comment was sitting drinking and seemed to want no further involvement, other than to keep looking in our direction and uttering what looked like insults. My lipreading isn't brilliant, but I was right, 'old slappers' 'f*****g tarts and others were being mouthed. I chose to save that girls life that night, and I never passed this information on to Jules, although at one point when I had to visit the bathroom, as I went past I told her to stop with the insults before I told Nana what she was saying about her! That worked.

We did have several scraps that season. It mostly seemed to be big groups of women, or just really big women! I tackled a mountain of a Russian woman once, she was intimidating every other woman on the dance floor in a nightclub we liked to visit. She was holding her own game of rugby I think, and when I responded to the third or fourth tackle on me with a comment, she dragged me outside. How dare she, how very dare she! I was however, holding my own, and I had my wing-woman standing by. But the bouncers stopped that one. She was made to leave! Jules and I were never asked to leave, as the bouncers knew we never started any of these fracas!

176

I look back now and see that we were actually doing a public service. And yes, I'm grinning as I type this! For all the people in life who take the mickey, who are rude and obnoxious, and especially the bullies. What they do is aimed soley at people who they think will not retaliate, not fight back and who will slowly skulk away. Hopefully, those bullies we met along our way might think twice. I hate bullies!

Who Stole My Car??

Jules and I were off out. Our normal nightly routine hadn't changed. Jules picked me up in her car, a tiny old-style Fiat Cinquecento. It was a great fun car, she even turned up on occasions with her son, who was folded in half sitting in the back! If you don't know what this car is, please check it out, you will understand what I am about to explain much better.

We were off in the car, heading down into Alanya town. This little car seems to run on tracks and I know you will be disgusted with us, but regularly we were both very drunk when we left town, and Jules would drop me off before heading home, which was a further ten minute drive away! I wouldn't dream of getting into a car ever again with a driver who has drunk too much. I certainly wouldn't drink and drive myself,I am not making drink driving sound like fun and I'm not recommending it. In fact I don't ever drink alcohol anymore.

But years ago in Turkey, it happened all the time, it was I guess like the UK in the 60's and 70's.

This night we pulled up on the same street we tried to park on every night. It was far enough from the town so we didn't get towed for parking in the wrong place, it was near enough to town to walk to the bars, and more importantly stagger back to the car at the end of the night. There was also a small shop on the same street where we would buy our 'drink' from.

After the car was parked, the night went as most of our nights went. We did our normal bar crawl, along the way, laughing at people and laughing at ourselves. We chatted to friends we had made in the bars and surrounding shops. And arguing with anyone who 'fancied a go', but generally trying our best not to hurt or bother anyone. We just wanted to drink, have a laugh and 'forget'. Jules had lots of things to forget, she had experienced a horrible incident in the UK which had broken her family into pieces. She came out to Turkey with her youngest son, a nice young guy who tried all he was worth to protect his Mum. But Jules was not a wimp in any way shape or form.

This night, we left the bar we always ended up in, and we went for a jacket potato. Where English people head for a kebab when they have had a drink, in Turkey it is either a jacket potato or a soup restaurant., All of this takes place at 3am – 4am in the morning!

As we wandered back up to the car, we chatted and laughed. We had a similar sense of humour and always found the same things funny so we always had a good night

As we reached the place where the car was, it wasn't! We both laughed and thought we were just wrong, we walked a little further and still no sign of the tiny white car!

What Jules did next would truly have made a monk blush, as she stood in the middle of the road, threatening death and serious physical damage to whoever had stolen her car if she ever caught them. I have to say I was finding this just funny. Who on earth would want to steal a car so small it would fit into the garage of a wendy house!

Not quite sure what to do, we sat on the wall where the car had been parked. Jules had a friend on the traffic police, maybe she should call him, as being drunk she couldn't really call the police to report her car gone.

We had been sitting there a few minutes and someone Jules knew approached us, he was coming from the opposite direction that we had.

'What's up?' Jules answered by explaining that her 'bastard' car had been stolen! He laughed, and although I could see his point, Jules didn't! He then stopped laughing and told us to walk around the corner!

We did, and hey ho there was the little car. Only problem was that some jokers had thought it was funny to have lifted the little car onto the top of wall retaining a sort of grass embankment!

Jules would probably have gone to jail had she ever found out who did it.

But at least we got the car back. Well sort of!

Running Away

Cevat had a friend he spent a lot of time with called Murat. Murat could speak English, and at one point Cevat and Murat were developing customers in the UK. But Murat was sneaky, I had heard him mis-translate things for Cevat. I had never stuck my nose in, as sometimes I wondered if it was for business reasons, and to avoid mistakes being made. But I didn't like him, and I didn't like the way he conducted himself. He didn't like me either, and neither one of us made any attempts to disguise it.

Cevat was quite entertained by this, but he did try not to ask me to help him with producers or packing factories when Murat was about. Sometimes that wasn't always possible though, and we did all end up travelling about for a day with an English man whose name left my memory years ago. We were showing him around a couple of factories. The citrus business was a bit of an eye opener for me, Russian customers wanted grapefruits the size of footballs, English customers wanted grapefruits the size of large oranges, and it went on and on. We were all looking for someone who wanted what we were growing, well not we, Cevat, but my wages relied on sales too, so it felt like mine.

We were in and around Dortyol, Iskenderun and Erzin. It had been a hard day, I tried to dress in a professional way but it was hot, four of us being in the car didn't help. We were all getting a little grumpy. We stopped in Iskenderun as I discovered that Murat and the English-man-abroad were staying in a hotel there. The Englishman was leaving early the next morning and we arranged to collect Murat after that.

I didn't know where we were heading, we'd been out a couple of days and I was ready for heading back to Alanya. The kids were away for a few days with Mum and Dad, but I was missing them. The guy we had managing the tour shop had texted me a couple of times asking when I would be back, and I thought there must be a reason as he was normally OK. He'd worked in the shop before Cevat and I took it on, but this year was turning out to be a bad year; war and lack of tourists. But the season was nearly over. I was in the middle of some sort of a melt down and was out almost every night when I was back in Alanya and Cevat wasn't there. I was getting tired of travelling miles with the Citrus business. I had wanted to put my all into the tour shop. I could sell when I was there, but the end of the season was approaching and I was once again wondering what I could do during the winter. I was making money with Cevat, but I wouldn't move away from Alanya and the citrus groves were ten hours drive away.

This evening was another of those back-breaking straws for me. Cevat had always openly talked about his wife, and I knew what he told me to be true. We had been together for 8 months, and never in that time had he seen her. He spoke on the phone occasionally, but even when we were close by he never went home. He'd said when I first met him that his marriage was for show only, and that it was really over but in name.

Cevat headed off the main road, up through a small town I'd never been to. When I asked where we were going, I got the oddest reply. I was going to a hotel, and Cevat was going home. Now I was 'the other woman' here and I wouldn't mind one ounce if he wanted to see the Mrs, but we had agreed a few rules and one of them was that I would never be with or near him when he did that. I know people who will think badly of me, but that's how it was.

I let him drop me off, I let him check me in, and I went to my room. I told him I didn't want any dinner and he should go. He knew I was miffed, but he left. I slept well and I woke very early. I was going home. As I walked through reception I told the guy that Cevat would be there shortly and would pay the bill. I asked him if there were coaches running to Adana, and he told me they ran frequently along the main road, and he gave me the name of which shop to stand outside to flag a coach down. I walked out of the hotel and back in the direction of the main road. It was quite a walk to the man road, it took me almost an hour, but I hadn't been waiting long when a coach appeared. I climbed onboard and sat at the first empty seat. I paid for my ticket as the steward wandered about, then sat back. It was about an hour to Adana, where there was a huge bus station. I could pick up a coach to Alanya and finally get home.

About 30 minutes into my journey my phone started ringing. It was Cevat. When I answered he was a little miffed. He was worried about where I was and he was annoyed that I'd left. When I told him, he was incredulous. How had I got to the coach, how had I found it? I didn't think it had been too difficult and I told him so. He asked me if Yusuf had helped me for some reason? Nope. He asked if I had argued with anyone, had Murat upset me? Nope. The phone went dead.

When I arrived at Adana bus station, I found the ticket window for the company I needed and bought and paid for a ticket to Alanya. I chose the front seat near the door. If I was lucky they wouldn't put anyone next to me. I grabbed a drink and something to eat then jumped on the bus. I had about 15 minutes to wait. But not 5 minutes after I got onto the bus Murat appeared in the bus doorway, out of breath and looking panicked. This amused me slightly, he was a big lad and had clearly been moving faster than his pokey little legs were capable of!

I was told that Cevat was in the car park, just parking up, that Cevat had collected him in Iskenderun and had driven like a lunatic to catch me before I left. I stepped off the bus and Cevat was walking towards me. We had a discussion about staying or going. He had a customer who he wanted me to meet with, he wanted me to stay another few days as he had 'things' happening. Déjà vu? He wanted, he needed, he, he, he. I told him that I wanted to go home. I wanted to see my boys. I wanted to check on the tour shop, it was getting towards the end of the season and the shop would need closing down and I needed to be seeking a source of income that didn't have me roaming the country anymore.

I climbed back on the coach, I was OK, I'd had a strange season, working in the tour shop, selling as many trips as I could, going on the boats with the boys once I'd sold the trips. Setting up the manager of the shop and travelling with Cevat and yes, I did make money doing that, paying my rent and feeding my boys were my priority. I'd drank heavily with Jules when I was in Alanya. I'd been scrapping with anyone who upset me and I had clearly been out of control, but by stopping in the hotel that previous night I had woken up. Enough Tina now. Sort yourself out, and so I did.

The coach pulled away leaving Cevat standing there, not happy but knowing he couldn't change things. I arrived home several hours later, my first thing was to go get the boys from Mum and Dad's. They'd had had a great time, more swimming and eating. Two things that made them truly happy. The following day I went to the shop, the manager was upset because he just wasn't selling anything. Those tourists that had been brave enough to ignore the Foreign Office warnings and still travelled to Turkey anyway had just about all gone. The streets were empty. So we both sadly decided to close the shop. He would be going home to his parents for the winter, so was OK, but I needed to speak to the guy we rented from, and pay any outstanding bills. This I did.

186

A couple of days later Cevat appeared at my apartment. We sat and had a light lunch and he was upset that I'd run off! I told him I needed to get grounded and stay with my boys and stay in Alanya. He already knew that I wouldn't move. I told him that as a relationship it had been good whilst we were both busy and making money, but in the winter I wanted to be in Alanya, I wanted to be able to see my boys and find a way to pay my rent. He said he'd pay my rent over the winter, he said he'd find me another nanny to look after the boys, but he missed the point completely. I said 'No, thank you, but no.

He laughed then, and said I would end up knitting again, but that when I couldn't pay my bills, he would always be there to help me. He left the apartment and I was sad watching him go. He was a good man, had he been a single good man, I doubt we would have parted at that point, but I was back!

The shop was closed. I was out with Jules one last night. A quiet and uneventful night. It turned out to be the last night we ever went out together. But now what would I do next? Whatever it was, hopefully there would be no wars or acts of terrorism to undermine my efforts again.

A Diamond Irish Lady

I met a diamond of a lady when I was working for Sun world Ireland. I was only doing airport transfers, but as we were travelling and after I'd done 'my bit' on the microphone, I found I was being asked millions of questions. Questions about service charges on property, about gas, electric, water bills. Where to buy furniture and white goods. It went on and on. And it seemed that the Estate agents were promising lots of help, but once sales were made little of it actually materialised. Before the end of the season I took a chance and had a few business cards printed off. I sneakily passed them to the people asking questions, and told them I could help if they got stuck.

I'd just closed my tour business. Cevat had walked away, and although I was getting occasional texts from him, we were both moving on. I had spoken to a friend of mine, a man called Abidin who I'd met previously. I'd met him when I used to hang about in his restaurant when I was waiting for buses to take me to work. His restaurant was open all year. It was in a great place next to the huge market which was held in Alanya every Friday. I asked if he had any jobs that I could do. He said he would find something for me, and my next job was to try and encourage people to go into the restaurant, and/or encourage the foreigners who came in to buy more of a Turkish meal rather than just a wrap or a snack because they didn't understand the menu. So I started there, he had said he would pay me exactly what my monthly rent was, so it was a start, but I still needed something else. However, I had a plan, the details of that will follow later.

Most of my hours at the restaurant were within school hours, and we'd moved apartments whilst I was with Cevat, so we were within easy walking distance of the restaurant. When the boys finished school, they could join me and Abidin was more than happy for the boys to have a plate full of staff food, which was always a good meal. When I went back in the evening, the boys would walk down with me, and there was always something to see or do on the way. They would sometimes walk down with me and then go around to the internet café. They were now old enough that I would dare leave them for a couple of hours.

But for now, I started at the restaurant. Long hours, but I could get people in. Some of the ex-pats living there would come see me, and on Fridays I did really well. I also made lots of new friends which is always a good thing. I was doing OK and my wages were justified. I was also taking people shopping if anyone asked me for something specific, if they wanted me to take them, I would go along with them and hopefully a small commission would follow their purchase. So far so good.

One evening when I was sitting in the restaurant, I answered my phone and it was a really nice Irish lady named Eileen, she reminded me that she was one of the first people I gave my business card to, and she wanted to take me up on my offer and use my services. OK, say I, the date was fixed and I immediately went into panic mode. First of all I needed to change my day off. I only had a day and a half day off, but this would hopefully be worthwhile.

First stop was to the car hire man, I'd been sending him business on and off for a long time and we had sent him a few from our tour shop during the previous season. I wanted to have a car, could I? Yes of course I could, he said. That was the first obstacle taken care of. I had no idea what Eileen would want, so I reminded myself where the Tapu office was, this is the office where property deeds were held and eventually handed over to the buyers. I found out where the electricity company offices were both in Alanya and the next town,

Mahmutlar. Lots of Irish were buying property there. I found that Water bills were dealt with at the council offices.

I visited shops, some I'd been in and some were new, I asked if commission was available if I brought genuine customers in. I asked if a good price could be given even if I was asking for commission, and everywhere and everybody I spoke to said yes. It had been a quiet season, and we all wanted the same thing. I was ready to start a new chapter.

The day dawned and I was off to meet Eileen. We had agreed to meet at the restaurant where I was working. Everyone knew where the restaurant was, since everyone knew where the market was. When I pulled up, I saw Eileen, her husband and another couple. I was introduced to John and his wife, they were also buying property, and asked if I minded if they tagged along too. I was more than happy. Eileen and I had already agreed that I would be paid 50 euros a day, regardless what we did. That was more than fair, and for me it was absolutely perfect timing. I'd get double the money!

My first day went fantastically. We were buying furniture, and this might sound simple. But way back then, before the property boom got started, furniture shops were few and far between, and they were tucked away on back streets. They also only spoke Turkish. Nowadays if you head to Alanya, there are dozens of furniture shops all on the main streets and other obvious places.

They hired me for a second day, and then a third. We bought general furniture, beds and kitchen furniture,white goods and kitchen ware, bedding and pillows. Curtains were ordered to be made. You name it, we had bought or ordered it. At one shop we were asked to stand up from the furniture John and his wife had just bought. They were just about to load it into their van to deliver as soon as John got home. Everyone was really happy with the service I had provided, the prices and the speed of delivery. The fact that, when the guys delivered the white goods and TV's they unpacked, fitted them and then took their rubbish away really surprised them. It was an amazing success, and I had earned a decent basic 'wage'. When I went back to the shops on the fourth day, I was amazed once again. They hadn't overcharged, but they were very happy with all the purchases made, and they wanted me to go back again, so they gave me my commission without any hesitations. When I got to the white good shop I asked if I could start a 'tab' and save up for new white goods I needed. He was happy to do that, so over the course of the next year I completely furnished my kitchen with Bosch white goods; a Cooker, a Washing Machine, a Fridge freezer and Dishwasher, the first and only one I have ever owned.

I had even managed to sell a car rental from my hire car man, as John and his wife wanted to explore on their last day. So, win win win.

I have to say, there is no need for an internet when you have good Irish customers. Within weeks I was busy doing this almost every week. Abidin was happy for me to go in to the restaurant when I could, and he said he'd pay me what he thought I was worth! He was a fair man though, and although I was going in less and less, it wasn't a problem.

I had finally found a niche, and not only could I do it, I could do it well. That winter, the customers were non-stop. I was finally making some serious cash. I managed to buy a second hand Renault Kangoo, and that meant I could start to do airport transfers, so during the night I would trip along to the airport to pick customers up, and a few hours later I would pick them up to go shopping or sort electric, water and other bills out. We went to my bank, which had a tourism sector and English speakers so that they could open bank accounts, and if they needed it, they could buy insurance.

There was nothing we couldn't find, or organise. I would arrange to have their apartments cleaned before they arrived, I could put a food hamper in their apartment before they arrived. I was smashing it!

They all became friends and asked to meet the boys. I was finally working mainly days, so during evenings we met my customers and had meals together. They would bring fishing gear out for the boys, or Bisto and bacon for me. It was the dream job. I eventually moved on to holding their apartment keys, and they paid me a small retainer every month to go in, check things over, make sure their were no outstanding bills, run the taps, air the rooms etc. I had 22 apartment keys at the peak of my exploits. I worked hard. On the whole, things went exceptionally well, apart from apartments purchased from one particular building firm, who you'll hear about shortly.

Never again, in all the remainder of the time that I lived in Turkey, did I run out of money. I was able to pay my rent yearly so I didn't need to worry about the lean winter months. The boys were happy and settled. We were doing great!

And it all started with a diamond of a woman called Eileen.

A Bullet In My Pocket and a Man Called Nebil

My 'job' with the Irish home buyers was a pleasant way to make money. They all knew me well, they all knew how I was working, with the commission, but they all knew that in return they were getting a good deal. In fact they really were, as the more people I took into shops, the better the deals got. The shop keepers were really happy, so everyone won and everyone benefitted.

There was only one fly in the ointment, and it was with a particular building group. They had built at least 4 or 5 apartment blocks, but they weren't easy to deal with. I was approached one day by a sweet couple, again from Ireland, who had bought a ground floor apartment in one of these blocks. They normally contacted the caretaker to arrange an airport transfer, but a few days ago they had taken advantage of a really cheap last minute plane flight and come out. They had picked up a taxi at the airport and gone to bed when they got into the apartment. The lady started crying as they continued to tell me that the next morning, they were woken up with voices in their lounge. Before they could get up to investigate, 4 people had walked into their bedroom. It was the apartement block estate agent with a family looking to buy an apartment. They were using this furnished apartment as a show house. The estate agent showing the family around was incredibly annoyed with the owners because they hadn't made him aware that they were planning a trip to their own apartment!

I did find out later that a lot of the owners weren't being given all the keys, even if they had been given the deeds. The builders and estate agents were telling people that they had to leave a set of keys. There were even cases of unscrupulous caretakers renting people's apartments out to prostitutes during the winter months, when the owners weren't visiting. This wasn't limited to the blocks I had trouble with, but was a problem with all blocks and caretakers in general

I explained to this couple, as I explained to everyone I worked with, that the first thing they should do was to change the locks on their doors. The caretakers had said it was in the case of fire that a key should be left, but come on, if there was a fire in an apartment with no one in it, then the door could just have easily been put through. Some people were also told it was the law in Turkey that the caretaker or builder should retain a key after the sale was complete. I asked if they would do that in Ireland. NOOOOOO would be the reply. So, why in Turkey? I upset a lot of caretakers and builders, but come on. They had made money on the sale, and still they wanted to make money from the apartments that had been lovingly furnished with personal items brought from Ireland, and use them as show homes to make further sales. The pity was that most of the customers I had, and most Irish people in general, would have been only too pleased to let people look around their apartments. But when they were there, not when they were back in Ireland without a clue someone was wandering around their apartment. The Turks got it wrong big time.

Anyhow, back to the original building group. I was visiting a customer who wanted to talk to me about something they were planning to purchase, balcony furniture I think, and towels and bedding. We were planning to make a list then zip off and try and find the items. I stepped out of my trusty Kangoo, and headed to the apartment door. The door was closed and I rang both bells, the one for my customer's apartment and the general door bell. The caretaker, who I had met before, appeared. He was a surly looking man, I'd often thought he looked like a very unhappy man who hated his job, but this day he excelled himself. He told me that there was no way I could enter the building. I was banned! I laughed and told him that people that owned apartments in that block had invited me. I had actually worked with three couples out of the same block. He really couldn't stop me. As we were standing arguing, my customers opened their apartment door and came down to the foyer of the building to see what the commotion was. They told the caretaker the same as I had. They owned their apartment, and they could have anyone they wanted to visit. Unless I was causing damage or a problem with other owners, he could wind his neck in and mind his own business. They were the owner's words but with my sentiments.

We carried on with our business and then we were getting ready to leave the apartment. I said I'd wait in the car. As I went downstairs and out of the block, there was another man with the caretaker. I recognised him as we had met before about a customer in another of his blocks wanting to install air conditioning. He had quoted a massively over inflated price, and the customer had come to me for help. Help him I did, only to be called everything from a pig to a dog! This guy was high up in the chain of command for this building firm, and in my opinion he was a cockwomble. He thought that even though he had sold these apartments, he was still in charge of absolutely every single thing that the owners did with them. It was outrageous, he was upsetting a lot of people, people who had spent a lot of money, people who were then becoming worried about doing anything in their own apartments without the cockwomble's permission.

The caretaker, who couldn't speak much English, and the Cockwomble, wombled across to me. He told me I'd gone too far this time. He told me in a very threatening tone of voice that I should step back and change my job. He had previously told me that I should be making tea and crocheting on the balcony if I chose to live in Turkey, or ideally f**k off back to my own country. But this time his threat was a lot more real He told me

I was interfering where I didn't belong, and that I needed to be careful because some of the sites I was visiting were still being finished off and were dangerous. That was untrue, I had never once been into an apartment when it was still in the building stage. But some sites were still having walls and gardens completed.

He continued by telling me that I could get hurt, quickly followed by a sinister 'Would anyone know where to look if you disappeared?' My customers came out at that moment, which stopped him continuing with the clear death threat he was making. I was shook up to say the least, but I got into the car with my customers, and we headed off to do our day's work. I returned with them later in the evening, and helped them carry the shopping into their apartment. The caretaker grinned at me as I did so. I was carrying some towels and asked him if he thought it was OK to have that colour towel. My customers laughed both at my comment and the face the caretaker made. He left, I finished my day's work and headed for home.

I continued visiting the blocks belonging to the firm the cockwomble worked for, but I was scared. I was in Turkey and a lone woman. It was back to the Man's world thing. They would never have threatened a man in that way. I had a plan, however. A few weeks later, I had some customers coming out to Turkey who needed help with a matter that meant we needed to attend a Notary's office to get some legal matter sorted. I would lie if I said what the matter in question was, but it involved cockwomble's company, and I had no doubt he would be there to make things as difficult as possible.

However, I planned to revert back to my 'need a man' way of working, and in this case he was a super special man. A year earlier, as I was undertaking my normal shopping and guiding duties with the Irish, I had put my good friend, Huseyin from the internet café, together with an Irish couple who wanted to open an Irish Bar. Huseyin was interested in managing such a bar, and his English was impeccable. They all got together and a few short weeks later they had opened the bar. It was unfortunately the same year I had my tour business and the 'war' slowed business down. But during the negotiations for the lease of the premises etc I met one of Huseyin's friends, a policeman called Nebil. I never did find out what exactly Nebil's job was but he never wore a uniform, always carried a loaded gun, and he could get anything done! Something like Special Branch, so I didn't really poke to find out.

I had Nebil's number, and he seemed like a truly genuine guy. He was married with a young family and had what I considered to be good morals. He wasn't driven by money as most people in Turkey seem to be. So, I contacted him. We met, and Huseyin was there to help too. I explained the trouble I was having with the building company. I confirmed that they didn't need a key by law. I checked if I could be banned from a building without a reason, and I couldn't. When I told Nebil about the threat I'd received, he was very unhappy. He told me he would sort it, and was planning to drive off to Mahmutlar, which is the next town to Alanya and where I was having the trouble. But I asked him if he could do it in a different way instead. I asked if he would come to the Notary's office with my customers, and just show his presence. My thinking was that this way, the Cockwomble would then see that I wasn't just a lone woman trying to earn a living. I was indeed connected!

The day of the trip to the Notary, we all met outside the office. As we walked in I could already hear the cockwomble's voice. These Notary offices are scattered about all over every town in Turkey. Many legal things are sorted in them, sales of cars, paperwork for divorces, they are essentially Notary Publics like we have in the UK, but boy, they do love their rubber stamps.

199

My adversary was already at a counter, having some paperwork stamped. We walked up behind him and said Good Morning. Introductions were made to the guy behind the counter. Nebil stayed back out of the way at first, but at one point during the proceedings, when we were waiting for paperwork to be read and stamped a million time, the cockwomble asked me who Nebil was. Before I could answer, Nebil stepped forward and introduced himself in Turkish, he was a very tall man, not overly wide, but very tall. He leaned into the Cockwomble's face and told him he was a friend of mine, a policeman and he did say his rank and job in Turkish, which I didn't fully understand. The Cockwomble seemed to understand, though. The transaction continued, but at one point, when only the CockWomble and the guy behind the counter could clearly see what was happening, Nebil put something on top of the counter and told me to keep it in my pocket and let me know if I ever needed him to have it back for any reason whatsoever. It was a bloody bullet! Ha, great, what an absolutely brilliant way of telling the cockwomble to back the f**k off me. I absolutely loved it.

It did the trick as well, never again did I have any comments from any of the caretakers, or the Cockwomble. Life was good again. In fact, a couple of months later the Cockwomble actually offered me a job! I think it was a 'if I can't beat her' situation, but I politely declined.

I was left with one problem, though. I had a live bullet in my possession and I was frightened to death of it. I never knew where to put it. Imagine, I had two young boys, so I daren't leave it at home. I didn't dare leave it in the car as the inside of my car sometimes got so hot I was frightened it would explode. So it was wrapped in cotton wool inside a small box, a sort of box that jewellery comes in, and I carried it around in my handbag. I was so happy when I was able to give it back to Nebil the next time I saw him.

Gambling Man

I was once again a single woman, and although I had gone through my melt down with Jules at my side, I did still try and retain a social life. Jules had by then met a guy who she seemed to be happy to fall into a relationship with, and I was happy for her. She was too nice a woman to stay as the angry beast we both had been that previous season.

Another English lady who I knew quite well asked if I fancied a night out. I said that if Mum and Dad would have the boys, she was on. Mum agreed, and I met Annie in town. She hadn't lived in Turkey for more than about a year, but she had money which made her life much different to the rest of the ex-pats in the group. She openly told everyone that she had met and bought her boyfriend, who then became her husband. She was a nice lady but we would never have been friends if we were in the UK. We would never have travelled in the same circles.

We were in town, and I pointed her in the direction of a nice little bar, upstairs from some of the shops in the bazaar. A bar that was easy to miss if you didn't know that the door was, down a small alleyway. During the previous season, Jules and I had found and tried all these bars and pubs! I should have published a pub guide to Alanya.

This bar had open sides with a balcony along the front, which looked out onto the bazaar area of Alanya and ultimately onto the harbour. The sides were open but without balconies, just window boxes full of lovely colourful flowers. Annie and I sat on one of these sides next to the boxes, ordered a drink, and settled in to listen to the singer. He was good in this bar. A good voice and he sang a lot of recognisable songs, all Turkish of course, but songs from the charts and not obscure songs that a foreigner wouldn't have known.

We were enjoying our drink and chatting away when Annie laughed and told me to look to my left. About 3 meters away from where we were sitting there was another club, but this one wasn't open air, it had windows down the side. As I looked up there was a man, about my age, maybe a little older. He was dark with a moustache and he was holding something in his hand and kind of waving it at me. I had no idea what it was, and to be fair, I didn't really care! But about 10 minutes later a little man tapped me politely on the shoulder and said 'this is from Hikmet'. He handed me the strangest thing. It was a flower, wrapped inside the clear cellophane that cigarette packets were wrapped in. I said thank you, and, as I could only assume it was the thing that had been waved at me from next door, I over and the man was smiling at me and I mouthed Thank you in Turkish to him. I then made a very conscious effort not to look in his direction again that evening, much to Annie's amusement.

Although I had stopped working in the restaurant, I would occasionally stop in for a Pide, a Turkish type of pizza. The guy in Abidin's restaurant made the best. I was sitting eating my Pide oneFriday afternoon. Because it was a Friday, the market was crammed with people. The season was over, but even with just the volume of locals it was a hellishly busy place. I sat eating and having a cold drink, the weather was still hot and I was contemplating having to step into this maelstrom to complete my shopping. My table was in the shade, and as I looked up there was a dark, well-built man. Well, he had rather a large belly, anyway. I recognised him, but from where, I didn't have a clue. When he introduced himself, it came flooding back to me, he was the man in the bar with the strange flower bouquet. It transpired that he was a very good friend of Abidin's, but he had been back in his home town of Gaziantep for a few months. His name was Hikmet. We chatted for a short while, and then I said I needed to leave to go shopping and thanked him for his odd flowers once again. He said he would sort my bill and that he hoped to see me again. I didn't commit, I just said it was likely as I came to the restaurant often, then I left.

I often had to walk past the restaurant due to its location, and I noticed that Hikmet and Abidin would always be seated at a particular table inside. Sometimes they saw me going past, and I got a wave. I went in with Mum once after we had been shopping, and a huge bunch of Bird of Paradise flowers were handed to me. From Hikmet again. Mum was a bit put out so I shared them with her! Then I had to explain that I didn't really know him.

To cut a long story short, Hikmet asked me out on a date. Now I say a date, but it wasn't really a date. Hikmet and I became mates, we weren't in a relationship but we were genuine mates, which I really enjoyed. If I wasn't working I'd go down to the restaurant and we would have a meal or drink together. He would stop us, and buy the boys meals too, if we were all passing by together. Once, he even sat with Mum and I and had a drink with us. He was lonely for real people, I think.

We went out with Abidin a lot too, and I realised I had made friends with men who were 'known' in Alanya. I had always thought that Abidin was involved with the Mafia, so it didn't hurt being seen out with him sometimes. Hikmet? I didn't know what he did, or seemingly didn't, do.

One evening, he called and asked if I wanted to go out. I did, and he arranged to get me picked up. It turned out he was another middle aged guy who had body guards or drivers, call them what you like. Just like Cevat, and he had a similar car, but his was a white Mercedes. I stepped out of the car and Hikmet appeared out of a nearby doorway. We walked into a very dark very smokey club, and I kid you not, a path was cleared before us, a table was brought out and placed on the side of the floor where the singer was. The table was instantly filled with nuts, olives, and drinks. I didn't have a clue what was happening, but it was fun. And everyone certainly knew him!

We had a couple of nights out, sometimes with, and sometimes without, Abidin. We became good mates. I knew Hikmet was lonely, his only friend seemed to be Abidin, but Abidin was married so didn't seem to want to be out constantly. I filled a gap in Hikmet's life I think, and he filled a gap in mine. I was going out, not every night but once a week, I didn't pay, which was a bonus, and we had fun. One evening we got to one of our normal haunts and it was fairly quiet, it was raining slowly, it was getting around to Christmas. Several people he knew were in there though, and a big table was organised so we all sat around together. One was the owner of a hotel, one was the owner of a car sales place, another was a nightclub owner and so on. They were all nice guys, in front of me anyway. At one point that evening Hikmet asked me to dance with him, as the singer was singing one of his favourite songs. The other guys encouraged me to accept and I did. As we were on the dance floor, they all wandered up and threw money over us! It is something that Turks do, but it was extremely funny. There were large notes and I was pulled between getting on my knees and collecting them all up and continuing to dance. I think Hikmet knew this and he laughed, and we carried on shuffling around. It couldn't really be called dancing. We then sat down and the bloody waiters picked up all of the money., They headed towards our table with it, and my eyes must have lit up, but Hikmet waved them away telling them to keep it! Pfffffff

I found out that Hikmet was a gambler, a professional gambler. Someone I knew asked me one day how I knew Hikmet, and I said we met through Abidin, why did they ask? I was then told what he did and why he felt the need to have a body guard. He sometimes had massive wins. And they told me that I should be careful, as it was a dangerous profession to be in. I had seen some of the consequences already though and now it made sense. I had sometimes bumped into Hikmet in the restaurant and he'd be so down in the dumps and unhappy. I had tried asking him what was the matter once or twice, but soon learned that he must have had his own things going on and didn't need to talk about them, so I stopped asking. At that point my life was going really well, and I would have helped if he needed me to, but I didn't want to take the weight of the world back on my shoulders.

But on all the occasions he asked me out, he was in a great mood. Once I'd been told what he did, it made sense. When he lost he was one man, and when he won he was another!

I decided that, after knowing as many men who gambled as I had, mate or no mate, I would only see him when he was in the restaurant, which I continued to do. At Christmas he sent his driver to my apartment door with handfuls of Christmas presents for me and the boys. He was a genuine friend.

He left for Gaziantep shortly after Christmas, and I think he was ill, but I never did find out. Being pals with a professional gambler was however, another odd chapter in my life. It would have been sad not to include The Gambler.

Why did I do it?

This was a question I asked myself for a long time. I remarried in Turkey and I remarried a man who didn't get on with my boys. He seemed to hate them and they hated him.

I met Fikret when I was busy with my own little property management business. His family were originally from Bursa but lived in Izmir, he had just left a job in a personnel office of a massive factory making jeans and denim wear. He was a smart man, he had attended University twice and his lifelong ambition was to attend the London School of Economics. He was younger than me by about 13 years which may well have been part of the problem, but I never acted my age and he looked and acted older than his, so we seemed to get on well. We got on well for a few months anyway, happy and working, but it was never meant to be!

This was a relationship that really never should have happened, and I don't intend to dwell on it. It has to be recorded as its part of my life, but it really doesn't justify a big write up.

It was one of the biggest mistakes I ever made. I met Fikret, and within a few short weeks he had moved in. Within a few months we were in the registry office in Alanya, getting married. He was a good looking guy and could be very polite and easy to like when he wanted to be.

Mum was unhappy on her own and I worried about her, so we all moved into a very large duplex apartment. Duplex means it was on two floors, so the apartment was entered on floor five. You entered this apartment on a floor with a few rooms and a bathroom, but then there was a huge staircase down to another floor with another set of rooms. Mum had a lot of the top floor, with the boys' bedroom and the kitchen on her level too.

Fikret and I had the lower floor, with an office in place of a kitchen. It was a huge apartment, it had great views towards the castle high on the hill overlooking Alanya, and it had views of the sea from two balconies. The complex had a swimming pool, and there was another similar block on the other side of the pool. There was a large wall around the complex, and an automatic gate to get in. It was a fantastic apartment and area to live in. Just a shame life behind closed doors wasn't as good.

Fikret was working with me, undertaking the night-time airport transfers, and helping during the day with the day to day services that the Irish needed. He wasn't however, generating any additional income, I could have done it all myself. But there really was little or no work locally for him. He really didn't like doing what I did, he found it a little beneath him, and he hated having to lift the baggage out of the car when there were men on transfers!

Aslan hated Fikret. He was frequently patronising and condescending to Aslan, and it was painful to watch. I spoke to Fikret about it often, and asked him to stop it. Aslan started staying away from home. A night here and there at first, and then for several days at a time. I was worried out of my mind. Aslan was sharp enough to be OK, but he was spending more and more time with the wrong crowd. I spent hours driving around Alanya looking for Aslan on more than one occasion. Arguments were frequent with Fikret once he realised that I loved my boys more than I loved him. Aslan had already gone through a period when he wasn't going to school, and he knew places and people that I really would have preferred him not to know. Adding a home life that involved arguing and being patronised was like adding alcohol to a fire.

The next unforeseen thing that started was a slap following an argument, I can't even remember what the subject of the argument was. But, oh no, I'd been here before, this time I fought back. It was vicious and every time he hit me, I hit him back, harder. We were in the apartment, but downstairs and no one could hear us thankfully. It was a real scrap, short but full on.

Fikret left the apartment, and didn't reappear until the following day. We then sat and discussed a break, or a change of some sort. We were not working together. My work was slowing down due to the problems in the Irish economy, he couldn't or wouldn't generate any further income. Mum had already shown that she was struggling with the hot weather even though we had installed extra air conditioning units for her, and the boys were starting to think and worry about having to do their National Service. Maybe the change or break was going back to the UK. Maybe my time was up.

We spoke to everyone and it seems that everyone was ready for this huge change and we put plans in motion. Fikret moved first. That gave us all a break from the horrible home life. Maybe when we were in the UK, and we could both work and earn, maybe the pressure would be off and we could make the relationship work? Fikret wanted to start his own business, and had spoken to friends and family and decided that the fast food business was the way to go. It was decided that he would stay with a family member in the UK who could get him a job in a kebab shop, because Fikret needed to learn the business from the bottom up.

He left for the UK, without any tears from me. I was glad to see him go, I was glad that I could rebuild my family and I had serious doubts that I could or would ever make another go with another wife beater

The story of our first few months together in the UK will follow, but Fikret and I were married and divorced within 3 years.

Interviewed in Dubai

This story is a trip to Dubai I undertook which was for an interview. The story begins with a friend of mine asking if I would ever consider working in Dubai. I'd never been before, but everything I'd ever heard or seen indicated to me that Dubai wages and a Dubai lifestyle would be pretty good.

My friend didn't want to go for the interview as he wasn't sure if he needed a visa to work there, and had plans for work in the UK. At this time Fikret was working in the UK so I was a little unsure, but said I might. I would attend an interview before I said yes.

Some Sheik with too much money was considering starting a travel business, and wanted someone who could speak English and who knew Turkey well, to help sell tours. I didn't know if I knew enough about the whole of Turkey, but where were they going? I could learn if necessary.

A couple of weeks later I was offered an interview, but it was to be held in Dubai! Mum was living with the boys and I. She said if I wanted to go see what it was all about, then she wouldn't mind. I thought I'd be mad not to, so I agreed.

Now I'm cutting a very long story short for a good reason which I'll explain later. I was given dates, I flew from Antalya to Istanbul, and then after a three hour wait I flew to Sharjah airport in the UAE. I was collected there and taken to a hotel in Dubai. The following morning, I was collected again and taken to a huge office block where I had my interview with 2 men and a woman, all nice people. They asked questions more about Turkey, rather than any academic questions. They advised that, if I didn't want to move with the boys and family that they could work something out such as working 3 weeks in Dubai together with a flight home for a week. The wages seemed spectacular, but I had no idea about rent, and to be fair, the company that seemed to forming on the whim of a super-rich man.

I was taken back to the hotel and given an envelope and told I would be collected on Sunday afternoon to go back to the airport.

I opened the envelope and there was a compliments slip with cash. On the compliments slip it said something like 'please take the time to investigate and enjoy the city'. I asked in the hotel reception if they could recommend a taxi who would give me a tour. I had found out that due to the low price of fuel, taxis were very cheap. A taxi was ordered and I had an hour driving around Dubai. I did say wow a lot as the taxi explained all the sites.

I headed out later that evening for something to eat, but oddly I ended up in a Turkish Restaurant!

I slept badly, Fikret was in England, the boys were with Mum in Turkey and I was in a place that I really, really didn't like. Why was I even considering it? I didn't feel bad that I'd wasted everyone's time though, as I had come out with an open mind.

I flew back to Istanbul on the Sunday evening, then had an 8 hour delay before getting back to Antalya Airport and a 2 hour drive back home.

This story needed to be told. It's part of my adventures, but I've kept it brief, as I really didn't like Dubai, it was super busy, not very friendly, and I really couldn't see myself living there, not for any amount of money. Maybe it's because I was on my own, maybe the hotel was in a bad area, but maybe It was just like my previous marriage; just wrong!

A Sad Goodbye

Once Fikret had left Turkey, Mum, The Boys and I were much better as a family. Aslan stopped running away and we all sat together every evening for a meal, which was a habit we had gotten out of over the past year.

Out of all of us, I do believe I was the only one who really didn't want to leave this wonderful country. It had frightened me, it had given me a livelihood, it had taken away a livelihood, it had helped me bring two boys up and helped turn them into wonderful teenagers. It had helped me prove to myself I wasn't as stupid as some people had led me to believe. It had made me hard, and it had shown me what a beautiful country of such variety it was.

I was leaving behind friends, a wonderful apartment, and a great place to live. I'd tried to buy the best I could afford, as my plan was to live in Turkey until I joined my Dad, and I thought I would never have such nice things in my life again.

I was leaving Irish customers who had become friends over the years, and I was leaving all the ex- pat friends I had worked with and known. I didn't physically say Bye to everyone. It was just too much.

I felt like a failure, as I had worked so bloody hard to just get to a point where I was giving up!

I was very, very sad.

Coming Home

When I came back to the UK, I was truly deflated. Fikret wanted to come here to start some kind of business. Mum was starting to hate the very hot weather, even though we had put in air conditioning in every room of the apartment! The boys, at that time were really not impressed at the thought of undertaking their National Service with the Turkish Army. I was the only one who wanted to stay, work was coming in and I seemed able to always find something to do to make money. Fikret however, really thought that running about for, or with customers, was a bit below him.

Fikret had moved to the UK several months earlier. He moved in with his cousin and the cousin's wife and their very large number of kids. They were lovely people, and incredibly kind to offer to let Fikret stay with them even though their home was already bursting, but Fikret struggled as he didn't like kids! He worked in a kebab shop, which made me laugh since he had thought that working with people buying property in Turkey was below him. Here he was now, washing pots and undertaking basic, and I mean very basic, work in a kitchen. He said he wanted to start and learn the business from the bottom up, which was fair enough, but still amusing.

Once we sorted the day of my arrival in the UK, he found somewhere to stay. He wanted to be in Newmarket as he had the cousin living and working close by, which would give him a better chance of getting either a job, or what he really wanted was to do, which was learn the business of fast food as he knew there was money there, but only for the owner.

When I did get to the UK, my marriage broke down fairly quickly. We moved, after a blip with a shared house, into a bedsit first. The boys had stayed in Turkey with my Mum until we got settled and found somewhere to live. It was impossible to just bring 5 people, including two kids, to the UK and magically find a home, work and generally pick up where we left off ten years earlier.

I landed in the UK. Fikret met me, and we stayed for a week in a rented room in a house in Newmarket. A friend of Fikret's owned the house, but it was awful. I freaked out when we had to use the shared bathroom. We went shopping for clean duvets, bedding and towels. But I was freaked out big time.

When I lived in the UK prior to moving to Turkey, my job was to help unemployed people to find employment, so I didn't intend to stop in this awful place and not work. I dragged Fikret into the local Job Centre. I looked for adverts for employment where no special qualifications were needed, jobs where basically anyone could do the work. I found one for a local laundry, which actually said no interview appointment was necessary, just turn up and ask. We walked round to the laundry as it was only about 15 minutes from the Job Centre. We walked in, asked for work, were shown around the laundry briefly and ere offered a job each. Start the following week!

I then dragged Fikret, very reluctantly, into a local estate agent. He was reluctant as the room in the shared house was cheap! But ewww, I couldn't live there, I just couldn't. We found a bedsit, and walked round to the building with the lady from the estate agent. The building was clean and tidy, and we checked out the flat and it seemed OK We were looking during daytime, though. Evenings and mornings were something else in that building! Anyway, within one day of being back, we had work and a place to stay. Before the end of our first week though, we had a massive argument, I carried out whatever I could, and went to a local hotel. Fikret followed, but a couple of hours later. He dumped the stuff in the hotel room I'd booked into, and then he went out for the rest of the night!

We moved into the bedsit on Monday morning, exactly a week after I landed in the UK, and we started work the same day, our shift was incredibly unsocial as we worked 1pm until 10pm, but we would be earning, so would be able to keep the savings we had longer. We hadn't accounted for the lady who lived upstairs, though. Every morning, at the time we really needed to sleep, her young kids would run up and down, up and down her room. She would shout and play loud music. This was every day. As we didn't get back until almost 11pm, and we needed to eat, we were late in bed and we really needed the morning to sleep. It was impossible, Fikret knocked on her door several times, but never once did she come to the door. We guessed because she knew why we were knocking. Fikret even asked the landlord, who ran a shop on the opposite side of the building to the one the two flats were in. She was simply dismissive. She even told us that the previous occupant of the bedsit we were in just turned his TV up to drown the noise out! Yeah we could so do that, when we were trying to sleep!

We stayed in that horrible bedsit for several weeks until we found a privately rented small house in a village a few miles away. We bought an old second hand car so we could still get to work with no problems.

To make the stay in the bedsit even more horrible, Fikret would go out on a Saturday morning and return on Sunday night. He said he was with his cousin in the next village, learning the business. But I didn't really know. I was stuck in the bedsit, we had no spare cash, only one car that Fikret was took whenever he disappeared. I knew absolutely no one, and even if I tried going for a walk, the bedsit was in the middle of Newmarket and I had no idea of my way around. Anyway, wandering around a small town was no fun at all!

I missed the boys dreadfully, and spoke to both Mum and the boys every week. I was so unhappy, so annoyed that I'd done what Fikret wanted and come back. To make things worse, the arguing intensified. I was becoming more of my old self again, through being on my own so much I think. I didn't want to take the crap anymore so I started being more assertive. As a consequence I was threatened a few times. The fact that we were in the UK slowed him down though, as he knew that if I called the Police, they were more likely to actually take notice, unlike the Turkish police. I don't tell you this for sympathy, I don't need sympathy, but I do need anyone who is reading this, and is in a similar position, to step back and look at what's happening. I'd already managed to get rid of one man who thought hitting a woman was OK when I was living abroad with two small boys. It can be done, you just need to make the decision. In the UK there is help available, the police listen and you would be the victim.

Anyhow, we moved into a 1 ½ bedroom house and I tried, I really tried to make a life. Not make life better, but make a life. We were still arguing badly, and twice he drove away and left me at work. Remember it was 10pm, dark and also cold if my memory serves me right. No buses, and I didn't have cash for a Taxi so I walked, first through Newmarket which wasn't too bad as there were street lights, but once I got out of the town the stretch of road to the village we lived in was dark with no pavements, just open fields on both sides of the road, and the verges were hard to walk on. It took me two hours to walk home. He was already home and in bed each time he did this! I would not be beaten, but he was such a smallminded miserable twat!

Around this time, Aslan was put on a plane by my Mum and I collected him at the airport. He was now away from all the bad influences he had been surrounded by, his years at school had finished, and I needed to get him on the right track again. I asked at work, and they were happy to take him on in the laundry. It was a hateful job, standing checking the pockets of dirty garments and sorting them into bins to go into the washing machine, but we was getting a good wage for a 16 year old. He never missed a day, never moaned, and I was really proud of him. He saved up and bought himself a desk-top computer. Now I loved it when Fikret went out. I was happy if he stayed away all weekend, because I had one of my boys home. Aslan and Fikret hated each other though, they always had done, so that was a little tough to deal with.

Life went on. I managed to get a different job paying more money and in the same village that we were living in, which meant I could walk to work. Fikret continued to take Aslan with him to the laundry, but I started work in the control room of a breakdown company. It was hard, I'd never done anything like that before, but the other staff were nice and I liked my boss, which always makes a big difference.

Life went past, not happy, I was missing my youngest but it was not so miserable. Work was OK , and it was great to have Aslan home. Fikret spent more and more time out, and when he was in we still managed to find time to argue. He had always been annoyed that I saved up from my wages to make sure that I had the funds to go see my boys at least every three months or to pay for Mum to bring them to see me, and I was at that time saving to get Kaan and Mum home to the UK for the approaching Christmas holidays. I was still paying my fair share of the bills, but he didn't like the fact that I was squirreling away money that, in his words would be 'wasted on the boys.' I was very lucky and had managed to win a bid to be given a housing association house that had three bedrooms and was on the end of a small row of four houses. I'd met one of the neighbours when I was waiting to get into the house to be shown around, and she seemed really nice. At last I would be able to get my fractured family all in one place. Fikret, Aslan and I moved into this new house mid-November. It was empty, and I mean empty, the family who had lived there before me had taken all but one of the light bulbs. These were some special kind of bulb, and it took me a few days to figure out I could only buy them on the internet. They also cost the equivalent of a small car each! There was no flooring of any kind, anywhere in the house, concrete floors downstairs and bare floorboards upstairs. Everything was filthy dirty and the garden at the back of the house was 1m high in wild grass and weeds! But it could be a nice little house with some work put in.

Through a friend, we found a guy who was exceptionally good at DIY and house painting. We, no I, took out a credit account at a local DIY store. Fikret couldn't get credit and he had said that he didn't really want anything in his name. I think he would have been happy to move into the house with only the furniture we had already bought. Kev, the handyman, did a fabulous job and I had cleaned the kitchen, the bathroom and a lot of the walls. He painted the interior from top to bottom. Apart from a pretty green paint which was for the room Mum was to use, the whole house was done in the same colour. A neutral colour which was easy to deal with when buying curtains and fittings etc. Kev also put a stair and landing carpet down. He put laminate flooring everywhere else and fixed a few bits and bobs for me. I was ready, apart from trimming the house when I could afford it. The whole family could move in as soon as I got them here.

It was getting close to Christmas. Mum was flying over with Kaan to stay for the holidays. I was so excited, and so happy when we collected them from the airport. However, it soon became horrible, the atmosphere was totally untenable. I was working shifts at my new job and I had to work Christmas Eve, getting home at about 7.20am on Christmas Day morning. The day before, I had asked Fikret to let me sleep until about 11am so that I would have had at least a little sleep before I started Christmas Lunch. I'd left presents under the tree, and climbed into bed. Not 30 minutes later Fikret started coughing and coughing. He got up. He crashed around the bedroom, clearly not giving a shit about waking me up. He continued crashing about in the bedroom until I eventually got up.

I was grumpy, oh so grumpy. I don't do well without sleep, never have and probably never will! I was up now so started preparations for lunch. The boys and Mum got up and we exchanged presents, Fikret was outside I think, I wasn't sure, but he certainly wasn't with us. It was not that he was Muslim, he'd shared Christmas days with us before. He did appear at one point though, to make himself two massive cheese sandwiches!

Mum and the boys were watching TV. It was about 2pm. I made Mum a Shandy and I gave Aslan a Budweiser. He was 16, he was level headed and I told him to sip it. It was a special occasion. 20 minutes later I heard Fikret shouting and I came out of the kitchen to be met with him standing over Aslan screaming at him! He'd taken the bottle from Aslan and poor Aslan was stunned and not able to respond. Fikret even had a few bad words to say to Mum who had started to defend Aslan. I flipped! I took the bottle back off Fikret and gave it back to Aslan, and I told Fikret to wind his neck in and if he didn't like it, he should leave! He went upstairs.

When lunch was cooked and I was serving up, Fikret walked into the kitchen. He asked which plate was his, and when I pointed it out to him, he told me not to 'put so much crap onto my plate'. When I pointed out that he shouldn't have eaten the sandwiches he lost it again and told me it wasn't the sandwich that were the issue, it was the crap food! He was lucky that he didn't end up wearing it. This seemed to be the way the holidays would go!

We all ate in almost complete silence and Fikret left the table long before we were finished. We relaxed, finished eating and I calmly went upstairs. Fikret was sitting cross legged on the bed with our shared lap top in front of him. He was smoking and looking at the ashtray next to him, that's where he had been sitting most of the day. I walked in and closed the door behind me. I calmly addressed him saying that he had not only offended my Mum, he had offended me and upset both my boys. I told him that I wanted him to leave, and I wanted him to leave and take all of his things with him before I got home from work the next day.

He did! That was the end of our marriage. It seems that I was able to put up with lots of things aimed at me, physical abuse, verbal abuse, being controlled! But start with my family and that pushed me too far! I'd kicked one wife-beater out and survived to tell the tale. I could do it again, and this time I was in my own country.

Mum and Kaan returned to Turkey after the holidays. It broke my heart to see him go, but at least I had Aslan now. Fikret did leave me in a lot of debt. The furniture and white goods we bought when we first got the bed sit, and the huge chunk for the house I was living in, but I spent the next couple of years paying all the debts off. It was easy to live on nothing, I'd done it before!

Early in the New Year, my heart broke again as I waved Aslan off to Phase 1 of his army training! We had been backwards and forwards to the Army Careers off in Cambridge. He had undertaken courses, he had completed tests and he was offered a position in the RLC, the Royal Logistics Corps. I was, and still am, so incredibly proud of him. I did think he would die or end up in prison when we were in Turkey as he got older. But look at him now, a tall, good looking, confident and hardworking young man. He was 16 and he was off on his own! I was on my own again!

By April, I finally had everything ready. I had completed everything we needed in the house to get started as a family, there was very little we could bring from Turkey so starting again was another massive task. I flew out to Turkey with very little hand luggage. The previous time I had been out to see them in Turkey I had found a decent guy with a second hand shop. Mum had been selling off whatever furniture, carpets and bigger items that she could. So most of the furniture in my half of the apartment had gone, beds had gone, bedroom furniture, dishwasher, and my desk and the office furniture had gone well.

When I arrived, I asked him to arrange to come over and take the remaining things. Mum had already boxed up most of the items that she didn't want to leave behind, and we arranged for UPS to ship these. The day arrived, and as the last stick of balcony furniture passed through the door, we walked away. We all had lots of luggage, Kaan was carrying clothes, although we knew we would have to almost start from scratch when we got home with him. Mum had clothes and personal items that she didn't want to leave, but that she didn't want to risk with UPS either. I had a few items of clothing, but I had cases full of curtains! I Know, but I had such wonderful curtaining that I could not leave!

We took a taxi to a small resort complex, half way between the airport and Alanya, and had a few good family days in the sun, relaxing in and around the pool.

When we stepped off the flight at Stansted which brought us home, I was once again felt happy.

Kaan started school, Mum and I settled into life, she found herself a little flat in the next village, I think maybe she now needed time on her own!

Karma is a bitch though, but sometimes it plays nicely. After the Christmas when Fikret left, he knocked on my door. He wanted to talk to me about his visa! He was worried that he would no longer be eligible for his visa to stay in the UK if we weren't together. I told him I couldn't care less, and to make matters worse for him, I was planning a divorce anyway! The colour drained from his face and he blustered and stuttered a little. I told him that I didn't care whether he stayed or left the UK. He still wasn't prepared to help pay any of the bills, but that's OK, it was my home now.

His parting shot as he left my doorway, was 'Well if you want a divorce, you can pay for it. I'm not helping!' OK I could do that! And so I did. I had very little spare cash so I went to the local court house and took some advice. I didn't pay for a solicitor, the only extra thing I had to pay for was a translation of the Turkish wedding certificate into English. Everything else I did myself, filing and paying as I went along. There was no contest, no complication about cash and no kids, so it went relatively smoothly and relatively quickly! Job Done!

The moral of this little saga then? Well.... A couple of years later, when David (you'll meet him soon) and I were living together, Fikret once again knocked on my door. Luckily for Fikret, David was away working. He started speaking in

Turkish, which he always had done with me, but I pointed out that we were in the UK and I would only speak English. He went on to explain that, although our divorce was recognised throughout the rest of the world, it wasn't recognised in Turkey because we had been married in Turkey. Oh dear, what a shame hey! I think he was worried that I was entitled to share in his inheritance!

He wanted me to go to London with him. He had a friend who could sort it! No, I definitely would not. Did I ever go back to Turkey? was his next question. I smiled and told him that if he wanted to buy me a ticket to Turkey, cover my airport transfer costs at both ends, pay for a week's accommodation with food included, then I would happily help him. He asked me why the hell he would do that, and my reply was 'Well if you need another divorce, you can pay for it!. That was fair wasn't it? He left with his tail between his legs

Ironically, David and I decided to have a week in Turkey later that same year. I contacted Fikret and told him that if he wanted to meet us one day, I would sign the paperwork he needed. He turned up outside our hotel and wanted us to get on a bus to go with him to the legal office we needed. Ah no, we went by taxi and David and I got out and left him with the bill. We needed photos, so we headed for the local photo shop. I went first, then I walked out to make sure he had to pay. Then it was on to the legal office. They asked a few questions there, had me write a statement and put my signature on a document, and that was my part done. Fikret was left with a lot more to do. This included needing to now go and have English divorce papers translated by an official translater.

Deal done, bad mistake of a marriage over and karma served!

Saving The Best For Last

Do you remember when you were small, at meal times, you would leave the best part of your meal until the last. Well I've done that with my life!

I've been married more times than a woman should be. But I have the man I was meant to be with now. My David. This man is my rock, my best friend, my lover, my protector and an absolute legend of a man.

Now, David's editing my book for me, as it seems I am getting too carried away when I'm writing. Commas and full stops seem to be like toilet rolls in this time of lockdown! He approached me yesterday and asked, 'Am I exciting enough, or am I boring?' He'd been reading and editing some of the earlier chapters and it was clearly bothering him. I was sad that he thought that.

This is David's story, make your own mind up if this is a boring man.

I was working on a service desk of a commercial vehicle garage. I worked for the same company previously in the control room, I'd worked in a call centre for a company who dealt with home shopping vehicle breakdowns, but I was once again in new unknown territory. There was so much I didn't know and although I was picking up things daily, it wasn't easy. I was also selling and arranging the fitting of tyres so I really was on a steep learning curve. But hey always up for a challenge.

The man I was working with was very experienced but he really like sharing his knowledge, and that was OK, I'd worked with people like that before. So I looked for other ways to learn the basics, the internet was a good start.

David answered a question I put on an engineering forum, I think it was about 'diffs' but to be honest I can't really remember was it was about. We became pen friends on the forum as David was happy to help with any random question I posed.   This went on for quite some time, and at some point David asked for my personal email address which I was more than happy to provide, he wasn't weird in any way!

We started to 'chat' on email, although he was, it seemed, very cagey about his own private life, and I was OK with that. I, on the other hand, had no shame and told David everything! We must have been chatting for a few months when I asked David for his phone number, wasn't it time that we actually spoke to each other!   I did know that he lived in the Cotswolds somewhere, and that he was an engineer, but I really wanted to find out what he sounded like. Maybe he had some super high pitched voice! Again David seemed to hesitate, but he took my number from me and said he would call.

Now I don't want to go into David's life before I met him, I don't wish to offend or insult or upset his family in any way. But David and I did speak on the phone. His voice wasn't high and squeaky, it was low and warm with very little trace of any accent from anywhere! Clearly we met, and we met one day before he was heading to Mexico for work. He was a truly, truly lovely man. He was going through a difficult time.   He was married, but not happily, and was being followed by that big black dog that I'd had trailing around with me in the past.

We spoke when we could, we emailed daily and we met whenever we could.   When I found out he was married it was incredibly hard for me, I didn't want to split any family up but I was well and truly attached now. At that time I talked to a good friend of mine, my hairdresser Emma, who was one of the first friends I made when I came back to the UK from Turkey, and who has remained a true friend. I told her everything, and she asked if I loved David enough to take what he was prepared to give me. I said I did, so that decision was made.

This is all a few years ago now, and for David, his ex and his kids it wasn't a pleasant time, but we are through that now.

I think the secret was out when I had volunteered to collect David from Heathrow, following a trip he had made to Shanghai. Whilst I was standing outside arrivals waiting for him, I put a status on my Facebook which went something like 'at Heathrow airport waiting for the love of my life!' Had a lot of response to that status!

David and I have been married a few years now , we still live, by choice, in my little social housing house which David is helping me to decorate and improve. We decided that we would rather have a nice car and more holidays than move house, but I want to tell you how we got here.

Our first mini break was in Barcelona, just for a day, and then we drove to Cambrils further down the coast for the rest of the week. We laughed. We laughed a lot, we talked, we even cried. We grew closer. Our first Christmas together was good, my boys, Mum and David and I. But it was tinged with sadness as he didn't see his kids.

For the next couple of years we both worked hard. I moved job once again, to be supervisor in a call centre. David, it turned out, only ever worked abroad. He is an engineer, and even to this day when anyone asks me what he does, my reply is difficult to understand. This is partly because I don't fully know what he does, and partly because the part I do understand is hard to explain. Basically, David solves problems. He is a very clever man. He won't accept that he's super smart, but if he wasn't then everyone would be able to fix things, and see things just as he does, wouldn't they? I've known him fly out somewhere to help with an issue that a company have had for months, sometimes years. They have usually thrown a team of engineers at it and still haven't figured it out. David rocks up, either on his own or with his business partner from Germany, and they find the problem in days sometimes! Really!

In between work we have travelled, long weekends mainly, and Christmas markets, we love those. We have been to Brussels, Munich, Amsterdam. We have seen Paris over my birthday which was amazing. We travelled to Edinburgh when Aslan was working up there, and we spent a lovely but very cold August weekend there. We travelled to Maderia for a Christmas market after I jokingly said it was a shame we couldn't find a Christmas market where it was warm! Well, David found one. We shot down on a toboggan in Maderia that runs down the roads, steered by two guys hanging on the back! We went to Vienna Christmas market. We went to Valencia, David was working there so for two days and I entertained myself with wonderful works through the park in the middle of Valencia.

We visited St Petersburg in Russia. Amazing, absolutely amazing. We walked in the cathedral where Rasputin walked. We stood in awe looking at the Winter Palace. I have never once been frightened when I'm with David. I have confidence in everything he does and everything he is. But he will be sitting blushing when he edits this part of my story!

Once David's divorce was sorted, he bought himself a super car, a Jaguar V8 F-Type convertible. We have a roadtrip holiday every year. We have visited North Yorkshire and Whitby, The Lake District, Devon and Cornwall, North Wales and this year we had planned to visit Southern Ireland, but this horrible virus has put paid to that, as it has for everyone else's holiday. Being in the car is such fun, we have the top open whenever we can. We laugh, we laugh, and we laugh some more.

We have visited Alanya, many, many times, I'm lucky that David loves the place as much as I do.

We had a super holiday in Italy. We started in Florence, staying right in the centre, and we travelled to Pisa to see the Leaning Tower. We then drove up to Venice. We walked over a million bridges during that stay and we saw many things off the normal beaten track. There are quiet places even in Venice during high season. And again we laughed, and laughed some more. From Venice we drove the long way, through the mountains, to Lake Garda where we spent a few days. What a wonderful place. Malcesine was a walk away and it was like a little fairy tale village with a castle overlooking it.

Finally we drove back down to Verona for the final couple of days. We stayed in a hotel which was unbelievably out of this world. In Verona, there is a museum with a balcony, and the balcony is said to be THE Romeo and Juliet balcony. If you have ever seen a film called 'Letters for Juliet' you will understand. But there is a court yard, entry is made via a tunnel under other buildings and there is a large metal gate into this courtyard which is closed from 7pm every evening. Inside the courtyard, hundreds of people cram in to get pictures of Juliet's balcony. There is a statue for picture taking, and the story goes that if you leave a note to Juliet, you will get an answer and it will bring you luck or make you happier. As you walk into the courtyard hundreds, thousands of these notes are stuck to a special wall which the council of Verona has provided for this reason. There is a special wall that can be written on, and again hundreds of messages in hundreds of languages have been left. There is also a special letter box to put your letters to Juliet in! It is a very special courtyard.

Well the courtyard became even more special once we realised that the doorway into our hotel was from inside the courtyard. The hotel was mind blowing, but the amazing thing, for my amazing life, was that after 7pm we could walk out of the hotel and be the only people in that courtyard. No pushing and shoving, no cameras in your face. We could wander around reading the notes and messages and it felt so special.

We went out for a meal and when we came back there were people standing at the gate just gazing into the courtyard. We rang the bell and the concierge from our hotel came and unlocked the gate to let us in. This miner's daughter from Yorkshire was truly astounded at that courtyard. For some of you, you might snort and think, pfff what's the fuss. But I will say for me... and being with David whilst all this was happening, was, yes you've guessed it.... Amazing!

But this is the one....   David had had a particularly good working year, and one evening early the following year we were discussing where we should go. As I came out of the kitchen David said 'What about the Bahamas?' 'OK' I say!

We flew out to the Bahamas in April 2017, we stayed at The Hilton Nassau, an old majestic building, beach fronted with a lovely pool, bars, little cafes, a restaurant, Everything you could possibly need. A ten minute walk into the town itself and sunshine, glorious Caribbean sunshine. Before I go on, I have to say only two things bothered me about that holiday. First, sitting by the pool one afternoon, a group of BA cabin crew, who were having a stop-over in the hotel, were on the beach. The only thing separating us from them was a hedge, so although I couldn't see them I could hear every word. They were sharing tips and tricks about how to not do their job! For example, how to avoid passengers without seeming to be ignoring them! And how to avoid serving passengers drinks, and basically every possible way to be a lazy bastard on a plane full of people (like us) who had paid good money to be on that plane. I was horrified and to this day I wish I had had the sense to record it! It is the sort of episode to go viral, and ruin a company who thoroughly deserve to be ruined. David wasn't surprised. He had collected three quarters of a million frequent flyer miles with BA, in spite of avoiding using them unless it was unavoidable.

The second incident also involved another BA cabin crew. David and I were sitting outside the hotel one evening. There were a couple of ladies sitting a few yards away and they really didn't mind everyone hearing them,they were really loud and had no shame. One lady was explaining that, although she wasn't cabin crew, her husband was the pilot and she had come out with him for a little free holiday. The other lady, who was cabin crew, had maybe 7 or 8 small bottles of prosecco in front of her, mostly empty. You know the type of bottles, the ones you pay through the nose for on a flight, or if you are in business class, the ones you can't get them to serve you! Anyway, these ladies chatted for a while, then another group of cabin crew walked by

The crew lady shouted 'oh, when you've been for your walk, come back to my room, I have loads of wine, ha ha. Well as many as I could carry off the plane with me, ha ha'! And that, people is why, if you can't get the attention of the cabin crew on the way home from your holiday, and you ask for a bottle of wine, why the answer will probably be 'oh I'm sorry we don't seem to have any left'! Shame on you BA and shame on you big time for your cabin crew!

Anyway, rant over, David and I were nevertheless having the best holiday. I'd lost a lot of weight before we went out and I was loving every minute of my slightly thinner self, but only because I found clothes to fit that I could actually buy! Great fun.

One particular day we were out wandering around town, we had been into our favourite bar for lunch, a bar where we could sit out on their upstairs balcony and watch the sea front, and where, across the way, we could see the massive liners that were pulling in and out daily. We liked to watch the people dashing off on arrival, but we absolutely loved to watch them waiting for hours to get back onboard. It reminded David and I why we would never try a cruise!

On the day in question, we came out of the bar and wandered back towards the hotel, stopping as we went at a craft market. Now, I love markets, and if the goods for sale are handmade, well then I'm in heaven. I went one way and David the other. I bought a lovely handmade basket which I planned to use for fruit when we got home. We headed back to the hotel. I dropped off the basket, changed my shoes and we headed outside for a sit in the sunshine and something cold to drink. David steered me to the beach which was unusual as, for different reasons, neither of us particularly liked beaches. Following David's lead, I kick my shoes off and we walked into the beautiful blue Caribbean sea. The liners were just pulling out of port, there were still a lot of people on the beach and around the pool in the hotel, and oh what a beautiful day it was. The sky was magnificent, the sea was warm and David was holding my hand. Had I died right there and then, what the hell, I doubted that life could have gotten any better! But it did! Unknown to me, while I had been shopping for fruit baskets, David had purchased a sea shell ring, and standing as we were in the Caribbean on that wonderful day, he asked me to marry him! How absolutely wonderful, and without hesitation I said yes!

He did later say that he would buy me a 'proper' ring !

My proper ring, well we talked about where we might buy a ring from, neither of us knew anywhere in the UK, possible Hatton Garden? We discussed it and came up with the idea that Turkey might be the best place, I knew lots of people with shops and we thought we might get a good deal.

A couple of weeks after we got back from Nassau, we flew out to Alanya for a long weekend. On the first day we wandered around the shops I knew. I had an idea what I wanted but hadn't seen anything that made me gasp and say 'yes that's it!'

On the second day we went into a shop I knew but only from customers and friends going in. The guy in the shop asked me lots of questions so that he could get his head around what I was looking for. He was very good at his job, and he soon starting pulling rings out of the shop window that were in the style of what I would like. I tried several on, and I was generally liking the styles that he was producing. During all this, he called someone and asked for a ring to be brought over to his shop. We discovered later that there were two shops who were in partnership. A young guy walked in, and then a large ring was put on the glass counter in front of me. It took my breath away. It was a halo ring with a beautiful stone in the middle, surrounded by several other diamonds in a square pattern. I tried it on. Most of the other rings wouldn't fully go on my finger, but I knew they could all be altered very quickly if we bought one. But this ring went on and fitted perfectly. It was almost like it had been made for me! It was fate! But when David asked the price, I quickly took it off and put it back onto the counter top. I went back to looking at the rings coming out of the window. David and I had never discussed price, and now I was embarrassed!

David picked up the wow ring and I put it on again. Whilst I gazed at it in awe, David chatted with the jeweller and he was explaining how they could take out the central stone, which was just over 1 carat, and put in a smaller stone which would make it cheaper but look the same to the untrained eye. I asked if we could go have a coffee. The price of that ring was eye watering! And now I wished I hadn't seen it!

As I sipped my coffee, David asked me outright what I thought, and I told him truthfully that I loved the ring that had been brought from the other shop, but it was too expensive. He asked if I would be scared to wear it and I said no, it was just the cost.

We went back to the shop and as we walked in David told the jeweller we wanted the ring from the other shop. The guy in the shop looked happily stunned and started asking David about the size of the stone he wanted to put in it, and to both his and my surprise, David said 'no, we want the stone as it is!' The jeweller rang the other shop to tell them he'd sold the ring they had sent, only to be told it had already been sold to a German lady, they had sent it just to show the style. It seemed fate was cruel and had played a trick on me. However, following a conversation with the other shop and then with us, they agreed that they could in fact recreate the ring, with the same size stone, and that they could have it finished in 2 days. The deal was done.

Three days later I flew back to the UK wearing the most amazing engagement ring ever. I had a mixed reception, some of the people I worked with thought it was lovely, and genuinely so, but although others said they liked it, I knew that they were talking about it afterwards, saying things like it was too big, or too showy. Most tried to find out the cost, but you know…. I really didn't give them a second thought. I was in heaven.

In October that year, David and I were married. We married in Gretna Green. This was another amazing day. I know I use that word a lot but how else can you describe this day. My boys and my Mum would be there too and Aslan's girlfriend at the time, a nice Welsh girl called Sophie.

I had given everyone an itinerary, as we were all setting off in different cars from different places, Kaan was driving up from home with Mum, Aslan and Sophie were driving up from Preston. David and I were in David's dream-mobile. We all met at a restaurant for lunch, and after lunch we set off for the last leg to Gretna Green.

We were staying in a hotel almost across the road from the Smithy where we would be doing the deed. David and Mum had seen parts of the clothing I planned to be wearing, but at the last minute I had changed my mind and bought a white-ish dress, which I loved and in which I felt like a bride. Only Kaan knew about the change, as I had given him the task of taking the dress up for me, and bringing it to my room once David had walked across to the Smithy with Mum and Sophie.

It all went like clockwork. David was off and I could see them walking up and across the road from my balcony. The hairdresser that I had booked arrived, and once she had left, Kaan appeared at my door. My heart almost smashed into a thousand pieces seeing him in a full dress uniform. I didn't get to see that very often, but each time I did I was so proud.

I dressed and picked up my bouquet. I had arranged flowers to be brought to the hotel. Then I left my room to meet the boys. And wow! Now both of them were in their dress uniforms. Shining boots, uniforms ironed with such sharp creases, and Berets on. They escorted me downstairs and across the road. People that were passing us on the road were pipping their horns and waving. When we arrived at the Smithy, we had a few photos taken, we had organised that as well. And the piper turned up. I would, just slipping off the subject of my wedding, recommend getting married at Gretna Green, it can be as complicated or simple as you want and there is a team that will help you achieve your dream

As we were getting ready to go 'in' Kaan said, 'you're doing well Mum for not crying' but as he did this, the piper started warming up and I lost it! I cried as I was escorted by two of the men in my life, preceded by the wonderful piper into the Smithy. As we walked into the Smithy, David looked at me and started crying too, and Mum was having a little sniffle of her own.

We were married over the Smithy, we had photo's taken, we went outside and had more photos taken. There seemed to be thousands, OK well maybe not that many, but there were lots, of predominantly Chinese tourists, walking around the Gretna complex and they started taking our photo too. Sometimes they pushed in so far that I'm surprised they weren't on the photos with David and I! I know Mum and the boys 'moved a few of them on'

We went back to the hotel and had our wedding lunch, complete with cake and table flowers. What a fabulous, fabulous day.

Since that day, David has become an incredible husband, he works very hard, he can sometimes fly home on a Friday and fly back out somewhere on Monday. That might sound like fun, but imagine all the taxi rides, the hanging out, the delays and sometimes the bad flights, screaming kids or plebs sitting next to you. Not so much fun when you've been doing that most weeks for 30 years. Last year, probably because of Brexit and all that involves, work was quieter. So David wrote a book, which has now been printed. It is a beautifully done, quality book, about what he does for a living. He followed that with a smaller, lower cost book, and constantly writes articles and is also planning a blog.

Last year we did the most extraordinary thing I could ever imagine. We went to New Zealand, and I was there on my birthday, the amazing holidays of a fat bird is another book for the future maybe, but New Zealand is probably the pinnacle for me. And yes here's that word again, it was amazing! The year before we had been in Paris on my birthday and I told David that he would never beat that! But a year later, on my birthday, I was standing outside the Hobbit hole where Bilbo lived! We were in Hobbiton, we sat in the pub where the hobbits had been, we walked around the village and across the village green where the hobbit kids had played. HA, beat that! New Zealand was something spectacular every day, something different every day, something amazing every day!

David has encouraged me to write my stories, I made excuses for a long time, but he was right. I am in lock down and have no excuses left as to why I shouldn't do it.

Remember I said he'd questioned me about being exciting or being boring. Well does any of that sound boring? Travelling is something special, but for the last three weeks, David and I have been on lock down, he's been painting and decorating, putting pictures back up, making doors fit properly, he's made scratches on my car vanish. He's working as well, putting proposals together. He's spending time marketing his books and they are still selling throughout lockdown, more slowly, but they are moving. We don't need to be on holiday, we don't need to be somewhere special, we don't need a fancy car and we haven't spent very much money during lockdown. He is still as exciting, still as interesting and funny, and life is amazing with David

I've never been bored since David came into my life. I've rarely been unhappy, and those times have been down to things that make everyone sad, like losing family members. Sometimes it saddens me seeing David worry, because most of the time it is completely unnecessary. So you can say that I am now very happy, very content and so, so satisfied with my life. We've had exciting times, and not always when we were on holiday. I am never bored, never! Even just being at home together during this lockdown has been exciting. Writing and editing this book with him has been seriously good fun. We laugh, we talk. We talk about anything and everything.

I have never laughed so much, ever, and that, my friends, is something to aspire to. No matter how much money you might or might not have, no matter where you are, no matter what you're doing. Laughter is, in my opinion the glue that keeps people together.

I love David with every ounce of my being, he is that wonderful piece of roast beef I pushed to the side of my plate to keep to the end!

Someone, in fact a few people, have said to me, 'Everyone needs a David!'. I second that!

And... if this book sells and I find its being enjoyed, there are a lot more short stories and anecdotes where these came from!

Printed in Great Britain
by Amazon